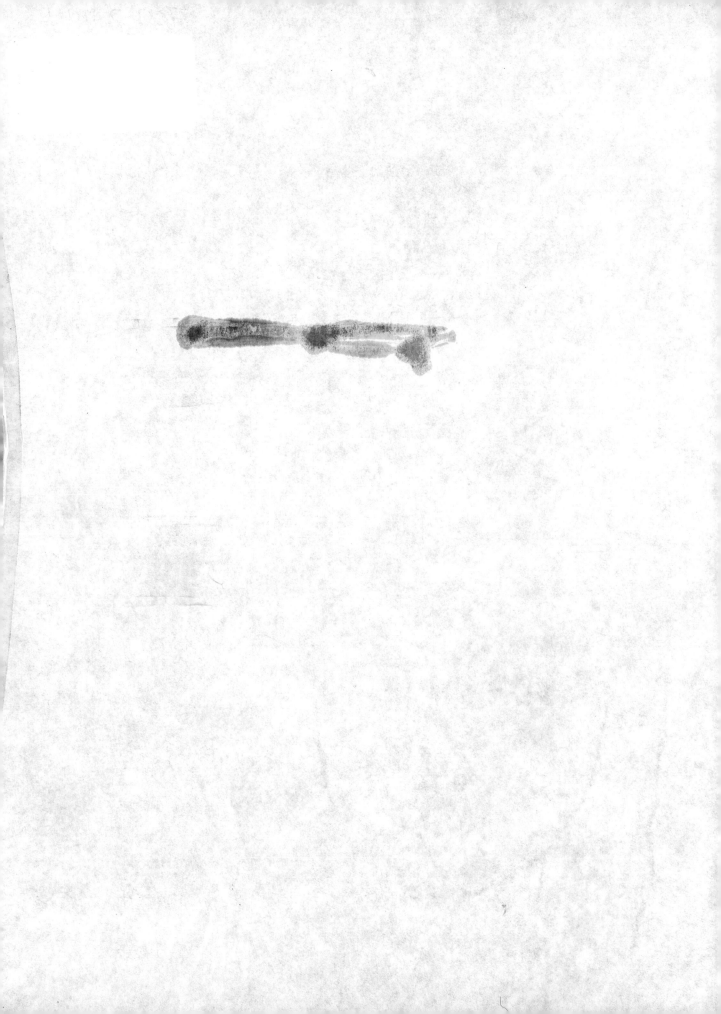

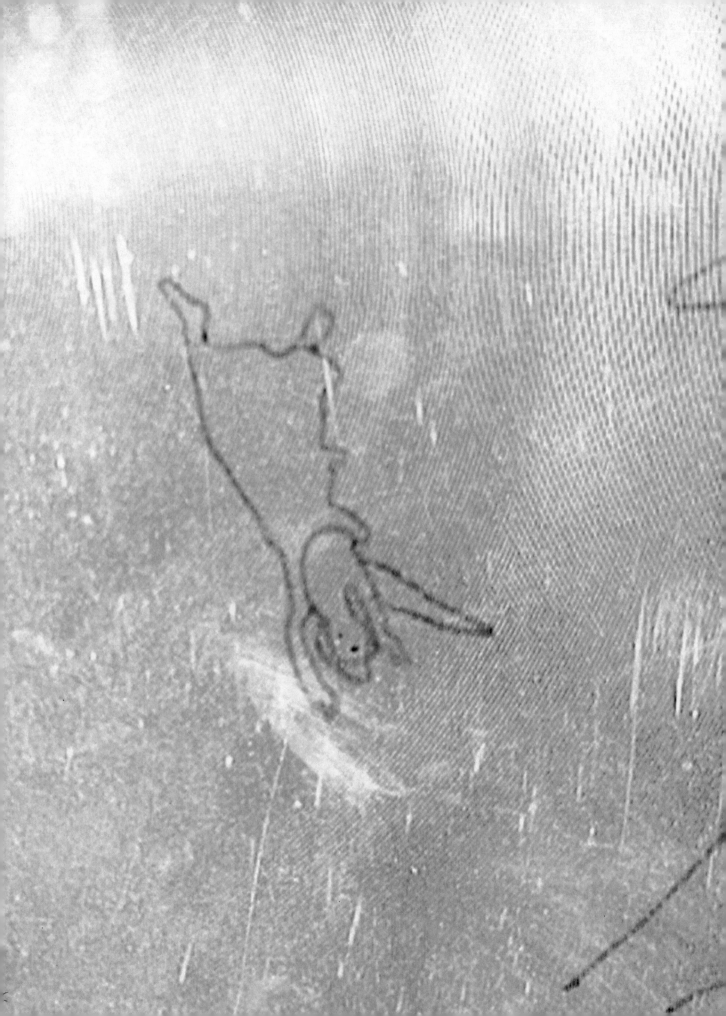

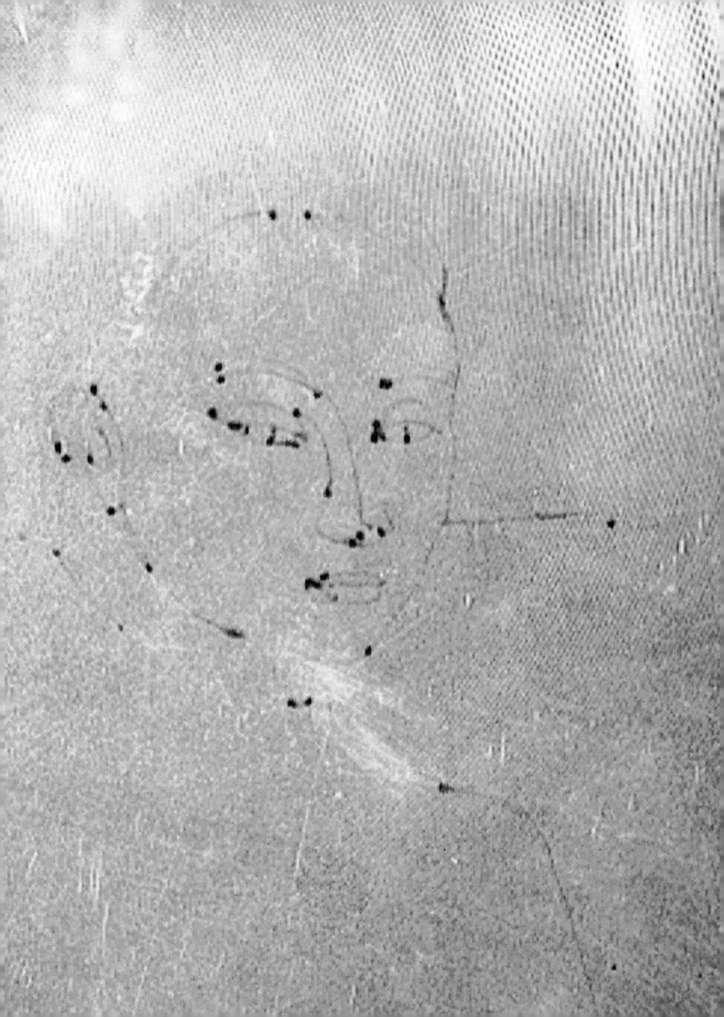

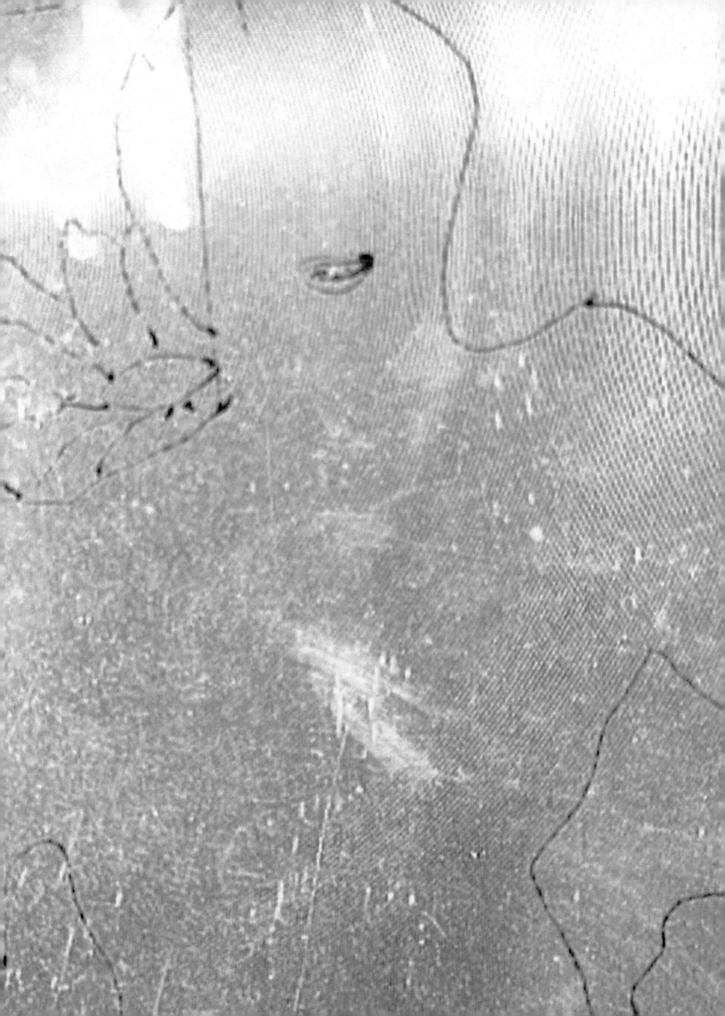

GARY HUME

BRITISH PAVILION
XLVIII VENICE BIENNALE

13 JUNE – 7 NOVEMBER 1999

THE BRITISH COUNCIL

previous pages:
Gary Hume
Selected acetate drawings,
1992-98
felt pen on acetate
Courtesy the artist

Published on the occasion of the
exhibition *Gary Hume*, British Pavilion,
XLVIII Venice Biennale,
13 June-7 November 1999

Published by The British Council
11 Portland Place, London W1N 4EJ
Distributed by Cornerhouse Publications
70 Oxford Street, Manchester M1 5NH

ISBN 0 86355 412 1

Catalogue © The British Council 1999
Texts © David Batchelor and
Adrian Searle 1999
Illustrations © The Artist
Edited by Clarrie Wallis

Commissioner of the British Pavilion:
Andrea Rose
Deputy Commissioners: Brendan Griggs
and Clarrie Wallis
Exhibition organised by Visual Arts,
The British Council, London

Exhibition Assistant, London:
Lizzie Carey-Thomas
Deputy Arts Officer, Italy:
Luisa Trabucchi
Press Officer: Hymie Dunn

Workshop Manager: Craig Henderson
Deputy Workshop Manager: Chris Hands
Technical Team: Tony Connor, Julian
Hodges, Gary O'Neil, Louise Wright

Designed by Peter B. Willberg at
Clarendon Road Studio
Printed in Germany by Offizin Scheufele,
Stuttgart

The Daily Telegraph

go

Wingate &
Johnston

FOREWORD

Gary Hume is a painter who likes to confound expectations. When we invited him to exhibit at the 48th Venice Biennale, he began to work on a series of nudes unlike any he had done before. Monumental, yet insubstantial, the figures appear to reverberate like afterimages, their pale contours registering against their backgrounds like impressions on the inner eye.

In another new series of works, birds are entangled in nests made up of their own silhouettes, so that we are constantly having to track back along the lines that Hume has thrown us to test the measure of what we are seeing. It is as if the painter is spinning a complicated yarn, in which mirror images, reflections, double-takes and reversals are all integral to the plot.

What's there and what isn't has been a preoccupation of Hume's, in some form or another, since the start of his career. From the paintings of doors begun while he was still a student, to the portraits of the last six years, he has presented the obvious in increasingly daring and radical form. Heads such as those of Tony Blackburn and Francis Bacon are brilliant distillations, enormously amplified. Familiar icons of childhood, such as the teddy bear and the snowman, are flattened out and painted in strikingly incongruous colours. Rabbits, birds and monkeys, normally confined to storybooks or to the borders of the decorative arts, claim a rightful place as subjects for painting, due as much to the panache with which they are handled as to their compelling graphic sophistication. Like painting itself, considered by some as irredeemably past it, or simply in danger of obsolescence as we approach the new millennium, Hume brings these subjects back from the brink, revitalising them and in doing so, reinventing painting as a live and exploratory artform. As his career has developed, he has steadily discarded the baggage of painting theory, freeing himself to take on subjects made difficult by our own attitudes towards them: romance, beauty, fame and emptiness.

We are delighted that Hume accepted our invitation to exhibit in the British Pavilion and thank him for his very good-humoured collaboration throughout the organisation of the exhibition. When we first approached him about Venice, he had already accepted invitations to exhibit later in 1999 at the Scottish National Gallery of Modern Art, Edinburgh, and at the Whitechapel Art Gallery, London. We should like to thank the directors of those galleries, Richard Calvocoressi in Edinburgh and Catherine Lampert in London, for generously agreeing to reconfigure their own programmes in order to enable Hume to participate in the Venice Biennale. The exhibition has been organised by Clarrie Wallis in close consultation with the artist, and we would like to thank her, together with her assistant Lizzie Carey-Thomas, for the unwavering commitment she has shown both to the exhibition's organisation and to this publication, which she has edited. I would also like to thank Hymie Dunn for organising the publicity and sponsorship of the project.

The exhibition would not be possible without the kind support of the lenders, to whom we extend our warmest thanks. We are also extremely grateful for the generous support provided by British Telecom, our exhibition sponsors, and by Wingate & Johnston, who are the official carriers of the exhibition. In addition, Go Airlines has provided sponsorship for all air travel relating to the exhibition; and the Daily Telegraph is the official media sponsor for the Gary Hume exhibition in Venice.

In Italy, we should like to pay special thanks to Brendan Griggs and Luisa Trabucchi and Marina Machelli of the British Council in Rome, who have provided invaluable help and advice and, as ever, co-ordinated every aspect of the exhibition on the ground in Venice. We should also like to acknowledge the support of the Board of the Venice Biennale and of the Biennale staff; with particular thanks to Paulo Baratta, Roberto Roselen and Dario Ventimiglia, as well as to Harald Szeemann, Director of Visual Arts for the 1999 Biennale, whose aim this year is for an exhibition that will be "a joyous event... not a retrospective reflection but a confident affirmation of the strength of the present".

Thanks too to both Adrian Searle and David Batchelor for contributing lively and enlightening texts on the artist to the catalogue; and to Peter B. Willberg for the catalogue design. We should also like to acknowledge the support given to the exhibition and the events surrounding it in Venice by Jay Jopling and the staff of White Cube, London, and by Matthew Marks and the staff of the Matthew Marks Gallery, New York. Last though not least, we would like to extend our thanks to all those listed separately on the Acknowledgements page, for their help in realising this exhibition.

Andrea Rose
Commissioner for the British Pavilion
XLVIII Venice Biennale

British Telecommunications plc is one of the world's leading providers of telecommunications services. As a company dedicated to encouraging and sustaining a communicating society, it is appropriate that BT is an enthusiastic promoter and supporter of the arts.

Gary Hume is recognised as one of the most significant British painters to have come to prominence in the past decade. BT is particularly pleased to sponsor this exhibition of his paintings in the British Pavilion and to be associated with the XLVIII International Venice Biennale.

With a market capitalisation in excess of £65 billion, BT is one of the largest private sector companies in Europe with offices in Belgium and joint ventures in Italy, Spain, France, the Republic of Ireland, Switzerland, Germany, the Netherlands and Sweden.

Dr Linda Porter
Head of European Public Affairs

Gary Hume
Snowman, 1997
colour photograph
edition 5/5
158 × 122 cm
Courtesy the artist

BEHIND THE FACE
OF THE DOOR

I am alone in Gary Hume's studio, surrounded by his paintings. There are images everywhere: portraits, paintings of birds and animals, a flight of dozens of angels. But at this moment my gaze has settled on a blackbird sitting on a branch. The bird has a yellow beak and his head is tilted so I can see one yellow-rimmed eye. His body is blue-black against the dark, jagged foliage and the branch is the same colourless tone as the sky. Nothing is happening and the painting has a feeling of perpetual, irreducible stillness and silence. Were it not so familiar, the bird would be almost heroic. It is like a child's picture-book image, only greatly enlarged. What is it that connects this everyday image to the others here in the room, and why was this image originally chosen – why this amongst all the possible images the artist could have invented, discovered or decided to paint? But more than anything, I ask myself why this image is so strange, and what it is that makes me return to it. It is the painted bird's solitude and stillness, the colouring-book plainness, the turn of the head, the beak just open, about to give song, that draws me to it. Like certain of Hume's mask-like portraits and even those early paintings which represented closed doors, the bird on the branch is a kind of icon or surrogate for something else. It doesn't reveal anything, nor does it fix the viewer with its regard. But it knows it is being looked at, and chooses to remain.

Gary Hume mostly traces his images from photographs onto a sheet of plastic or acetate, lays the translucent sheet on the underlit bed of an epidiascope and projects the tracing onto the surface of the painting's aluminium support. He then retraces the projected line-drawing. The addition of colour is equally automatic, a matter of filling-in. His images are purged of inessentials. Until around 1997 his paintings were almost entirely constructed from flat planes and shapes. The under-drawing functioned as a contour for the mapping of these edges and planes – drawing which contains and divides. The paint itself has the same plain, declarative feel, doesn't hold brush-strokes, and dries smooth and glossy. It has a brittle, shimmering glamour. As one moves about the paintings real light and shadows smear the surface in blurry reflection. "I don't use light", Hume has said, "because that would be like painting space, so I used gloss paint to reflect light, to take real light. In my studio, which is a daylight studio, the paintings are shifting constantly". The colours Hume uses are the colours of modern urban life, the colours of cars, products and posters, colours which go in and out of fashion, colours which shine with an artificial brilliance, and will one day bleach-out and die. They are shrill and chemical, but also oddly fugitive and unnatural. They catch the vividness of the passing moment.

The line appears where the paint leaves off. In recent paintings Hume's line has become more autonomous. Drawing is now more like a cut through the surface. The ground shines through, the shine of the bare aluminium under the paint. The line is an incision. This unpainted line has a frozen quality, a feeling of energy held in suspension. Unlike a directly drawn freehand line, it has no sense of speed or attack. Its width and weight are controlled exactly, the accidental hooks and skids fixed and equalised with a kind of impassiveness, which gives even the most playful image-making a peculiar authority and gravitas. This de-personalised line, coupled with Hume's insistently flat colour, can be unnerving.

Unlike the drawn comic-book outlines in early paintings by his compatriot Patrick Caulfield, which build an illusionary space on an uninflected coloured ground, line in Hume's recent paintings does something different, and will not submit to being sculpted by the eye. In Caulfield's work, the drawing describes a conventional, usually architectural space, setting the viewer's brain to work on the indisputable flatness of the coloured ground, which one involuntarily folds into three dimensions. The artist sets up familiar cues, so that one knows how to read the image without having to think about it. This is Caulfield's 'transparency', and the transparency within many paintings of David Salle (which only recomplicated Francis Picabia's poetic device), as well as the transparency of the paintings and wall drawings of Michael Craig-Martin. Instead, you shuttle back and forth across the surface of Hume's paintings, making and unmaking form. Perhaps the illusion of space is unavoidable, and has something

Patrick Caulfield
Inside a Swiss Chalet, 1969
oil on canvas
276.9 × 182.9 cm
Waddington Galleries, London
© Patrick Caulfield 1999

Gary Hume
Song, 1998
gloss paint on aluminium panel
208.5 × 117 cm
Courtesy Jay Jopling, London

to do with the ways our brains are wired. We divide the world into figure and ground, presence and absence. In the recent *Song* paintings, this becomes difficult. If any of Hume's paintings get beneath the surface of things, it is these. The *Song* paintings are a little like a section through a torso, showing spine and ribcage, or a view of flesh and bone in the larynx, for example, though this is all handled with such undivided attention to the autonomy of interpenetrating shapes that the configuration sometimes loses its grip on the model that inspired it.

A few winters ago Hume and a friend built a snowman on a hill in the Peak District, in the north of England. They coloured the snow with food dye and took photographs of it. The snowman ended up as a painting, *Snowman,* 1996, the object reduced to a small tan coloured circle resting on a larger red circle, set against a cold blue and grey background. Without the title, one would barely be aware of what the painting represents, and certainly not the building of the actual coloured snowman that led up to it. But the painting is more than a wistful and poetic reminder of a day's lark in the cold,

Gary Hume
Monkey, 1997
gloss paint on aluminium panel
89 × 82.5 cm
The British Council, London

La Dame à la licorne – La Vue (detail)
Paris Musée National du Moyen-Age,
Thermes et Hôtel de Cluny
© Caroline Rose

although in a sense it is a souvenir. What is particularly interesting about the painting is that once one has read the title the painting becomes the snowman, and it is difficult to read it any other way.

Looking at Hume's paintings, I sometimes experience a kind of déja vu: suddenly I'm back in the 1960s, in a world of second generation post-painterly abstractionists. Then in a children's nursery, hung with mobiles and colouring book animals. But does a painting like *Polar Bear*, 1994, belong in a nursery? This opened-out, green, teddy-bear shape isn't as benign as it looks. Nor are the animals in the *Garden Paintings*, 1996, whose images are drawn from a group of fifteenth century French tapestries, *La Dame à la licorne*. Hume has kept remarkably close to the original, yet the paintings are anything but a mechanical or anonymous transposition. The animals are disquieting. They seem to be waiting, and watching. Hume's *Snowman* is like this too, and if we think of it as a portrait, then we have found ourselves standing behind the figure, looking for a face that we will never see.

What remains is a strangeness, a sense of things frozen and suspended in the painting's silence: an owl sitting on a branch, a rabbit munching a leaf, a closed door, bare feet on black grass, a face. Hume's paintings sometimes allude to feelings – *Scared, Begging For It, Fear, Poor Thing* – but they don't explain those feelings, nor do they illustrate them. Hume's paintings present us with arrested images.

For a long time, Hume only painted doors – life-sized, one colour paintings whose proportions and details were measured directly from

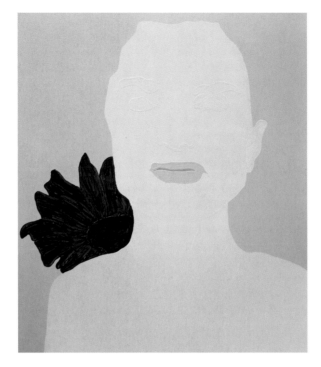

Gary Hume
Adult, 1994
gloss paint on MDF panel
147.6 × 124.7 cm
Carol & Arthur Goldberg Collection

Gary Hume
Rabbit and Flowers, 1996
gloss paint on aluminium panel
76.8 × 57.1 cm
Courtesy Galerie Aurel Scheibler, Cologne

real institutional doors – which were painted just as real doors are painted, in slick, shiny household gloss paint. The door, the artist said, "looked like a face, which I liked straight away, and it also looked like perfect modernism". Hume's *Door Paintings* performed a neat coalescence of the painted image and the things they represented. The paintings resembled doors but were not doors, and like Hume's *Snowman*, we were on the wrong side of them. These were the kinds of doors one finds in hospitals, opening onto an operating theatre or to a morgue, or perhaps on to a vast mass-catering kitchen. Whatever you imagined lay on the other side, even if it was some kind of institutionalised heaven, the paintings left you feeling that you didn't want to go there. The faces one discerned in their internal configuration of low-relief details, the round windows and recessed panels, were a constant reminder of the difference between the painted and the real.

The *Door Paintings* recall a work by Sigmar Polke called *Schrank*, painted in 1963. *Schrank*, with its central, Newmanesque vertical zip and funny little keyholes to either side, more resembled the doors to a cupboard than the door to an institutional room or to the outside world. *Schrank* is a painting which has me fumbling in my pockets for a key each time I look at a reproduction of it, whereas Hume's doors have precisely the opposite effect. Curiosity about what lies on the other side of the door is tempered by the certainty that behind the painted door there is only a wall. Is it possible to think of a door and not think about where it leads to? The door was closed, and looked, too, like yet another figuration of modernism's closure, even

Gary Hume
Patsy Kensit, 1994
gloss paint on MDF panel
208 × 117 cm
Private collection, London

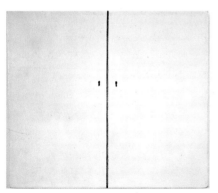

Sigmar Polke
Schrank, 1963
varnish on canvas
40 × 50 cm
Courtesy Galerie Michael Werner,
Cologne and New York
© Sigmar Polke

painting's closure. The first *Door Paintings* were painted with that ubiquitous magnolia off-white that finds its way throughout modern interiors, but the colour soon shifted register, and became bright, luscious, sensual and complex. Where one might have expected inert arrangements of bureaucratic creams and browns, or dead greens and scuffed blacks which are such a daily insult to pleasure, there were pinks and golden tans, and paintings in which the panels and roundels, the hand and foot-plates of the doors were picked-out garishly, or like exercises from Joseph Albers, or in approximation of the close-toned paintings of Ad Reinhard. Like Picabia's early watercolour, *Radio-Concerts*, 1922, with its symmetrical arrangement of geometric forms, loosely resembling the dials and knobs on an early radio set, Hume's paintings had a disquieting, robotic anthropomorphism which their artificial brightness did nothing to disguise.

Hume abandoned the door paintings in 1993. He even titled one painting after his disenchantment, calling it *More Fucking Values*, to suggest that all he was doing, from painting to painting, was to

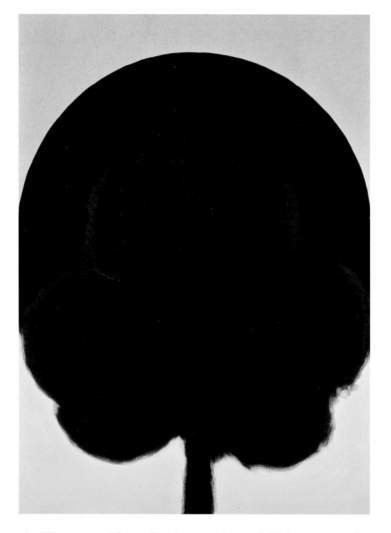

Gary Hume
Tony Blackburn, 1994
gloss and matt paint on MDF panel
193 × 137 cm
The Saatchi Gallery, London

Francis Picabia,
Radio-concerts, 1922
watercolour, pencil
and black ink on paper
73 × 59.7 cm
Museum Boijmans
Van Beuningen, Rotterdam
© ADAGP, Paris and DACS 1999

shuffle a set of formal values and possibilities over and over again. This was not a 'perfect modernism', but slavery. Behind the imperturbable blankness of the door lay a waiting-room, a room full of people waiting to get out: minor tabloid celebrity Patsy Kensit, with a sticky pink face and green lips, sucking her thumb; radio disc-jockey Tony Blackburn, who spilled his sadness out on-air; a man whistling in the dark, and a whole crowd of impossibly muscled figures. (These were derived from statues for a stadium in Rome designed during Italy's Fascist period.) In the painting *Jealousy and Passion*, 1993, one of these bulky, awkward beings has a lipsticked female smile stuck on his face – the same smile that Willem de Kooning snipped from a Camel cigarette ad in 1949, and glued to his *Study for Woman* in 1950. Instead of de Kooning's hysterical woman, Hume's figure is a muscle-bound yellow silhouette, wearing only that transvestite smile.

The shift which occurred in Hume's painting in 1993 came as a shock. The artist had abandoned the one concept which had sustained him.

"My art education was based upon the notion of having an idea and then being able to act on it and make something concrete... I searched for another idea and found I had no ideas... It was terrible... So I asked myself what is it I want? I wanted air in my lungs and I wanted a sense of roots."

Hume's response to this crisis was to make a number of improvised sculptures in his studio, using his young son's playroom slide, plastic dolls, rubbish bags, adhesive tape and plastic tubing. It was all, he told me at the time, about birth. It was more about rebirth, an adult's return to messy, infantile play. Hume had a video made of himself sitting, fully clothed, in an old zinc bathtub in the yard behind his studio. In his comedic home video *Me as King Cnut*, Hume sits in the bath, smoking and wearing a Burger King paper crown on his head. *Me As King Cnut* is, of course, the artist as King Cunt. Like the ribald play-acting of Gilbert & George ('George the Shit and Gilbert the Cunt'), it was an aggressively banal and self-denigrating piece of theatre. If the artist had to appear at all, he had to appear as a parody of himself.

far left: Gary Hume
Jealousy and Passion, 1993
gloss paint, pencil, cardboard
on MDF panel
201 × 133 cm
The Saatchi Gallery, London

left: Gary Hume
Hero, 1993
gloss paint on formica panel
201 × 133 cm
Private collection, London

right: Gary Hume
Roots, 1993
gloss paint on formica panel
218.5 × 183 cm
Courtesy the artist

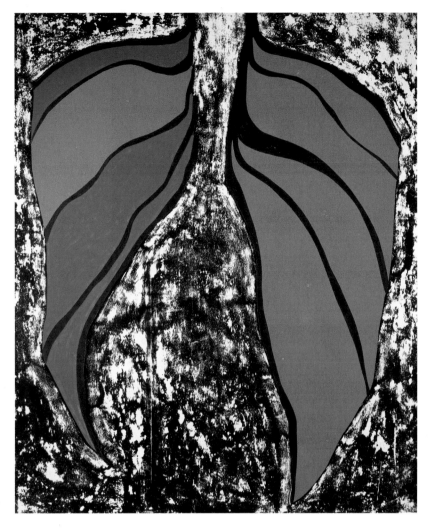

'What to paint?' remains a question and further, 'What is fit to paint?' Asked whether he regards himself as a figurative artist, Hume has said "I do flora, fauna and portraiture". It's true: Hume paints flowers, animals and people. He paints living things, or things which look as though they might be alive, but aren't really. His models include the concrete angels suspended from the ceiling in Oscar Niemeyer's cathedral in Brasília, a bird on a branch in a picture book, the bestiary in a tapestry. He paints the people he knows and images of people whose faces he has seen only in photographs and in paintings. He has worked from Holbein and from the obituary photograph of the dead comedian Peter Cook. Hume has said that he is an artist without ideas. (Not having ideas is, of course, itself an idea.) He painted a Madonna in 1993 "because she has been painted so beautifully". Because she has been painted so beautifully: this was the test. What could Hume do with the subject, avoiding sentimentality, avoiding a pastiche of all the paintings of the Madonna, avoiding invidious comparison? Hume's *Madonna* is disconcertingly featureless, as plain as the surface of one of his doors. Her head is

Gary Hume
Madonna, 1993
gloss paint on formica panel
208 × 140 cm
Private collection, London

an irregular black ovoid painted in high-gloss household paint, as is
the head of the infant Jesus whom she cradles. The Madonna's hair
flows through the painting in ropes of white. Hume liked the idea
that viewers of the painting could see their own dim reflections in the
faces of Mary and baby Jesus. Later, Hume went on to paint a
portrait, copied from a newspaper photograph, of a little deaf boy;
an otherwise ordinary boy in a striped blue shirt leaning forward
into the frame. Hume painted the anonymous child surrounded by a
halo, and called the painting *Messiah*, 1998. Hume says he hates
stories in paintings, but the possibility of narrative is there nonetheless. What we get instead is a painted situation, something stilled
at a particular moment, something enigmatic and inexplicable,
something as fleeting as a look, endlessly arrested.

    After Vermeer, 1995, takes the *Portrait of a Young Woman*, 1666-67,
by Vermeer, reverses her and repaints her in orange, leaving her
mouth and eyes, her ear and earring white. Vermeer's portrait depicts
a sitter who appears to be turning as though to welcome our arrival,
at the very moment that we come to her. She engages our complicity

Gary Hume
After Vermeer, 1995
gloss paint on aluminium panel
198 × 122 cm
Private collection,
courtesy Jay Jopling, London

in looking and being looked at with a painted suddenness. When
Hume painted supermodel Kate Moss he left her face unpainted,
sanded it down to the bare shiny aluminium of the painting's support.
A temporary, faceless Venus, she is a collection of positive and
negative shapes. She's there and she's not there, in her bikini, posing
her supermodel pose, with a little collaged-on curlicue, a delicate
paper wave, lapping beneath her. *Kate*, 1996, recalls a Matisse
cut-out. Not only is there an actual collaged element, but the rest of
the painting's hard-edged shapes have the kind of angularity
associated with the sheared arcs and slices made by scissors. This in
itself is typical: Hume's outline describes and isolates forms, or parts
of forms, rather than bringing them together. He maps the surface,
the topography, and colours-in areas just as one would colour a map.
The solidity of form and mass has been replaced by a topographical
perspective, what Hume calls a "God's eye view". You feel you could
reach out and peel off a painted flower, or an ear, or an eye, and
hold it up between finger and thumb, where it would have no more
substance and thickness than the layer of paint it is made from.

Gary Hume
After Petrus Christus, 1995
gloss paint on MDF panel
38.5 × 28.5 cm
Mrs Jill Henshaw

Hume's portrait of Francis Bacon, *Francis*, 1997, looks as if Bacon is wearing an orange ski-mask, or a terrorist's balaclava, or as if he had spent rather too long on a sun bed. Hume painted Bacon with a few mad hairs springing from his head and tiny teeth bared between thin red lips, as a somewhat alarming but humorous cypher, as if to debunk Bacon's ghostly presence as a kind of Brando-esque Godfather to current British art. Or rather, to prick the overly reverential attitude which surrounds Bacon's reputation, while at the same time looking over his shoulder to him, just as Bacon looked back at, and painted, the death mask of William Blake.

Often, Hume's portraits are reduced to an instantaneous look or glance – he freezes that sudden apprehension of a pair of eyes, hair, that blob on a stalk for a head on a neck. Hume's portraits are often about such fleeting moments of recognition, yet the more one looks the more complex these paintings become. They are portraits painted in the subject's absence, representing not so much the person as the space that their body would occupy, the trace of a portrait, a barely fleshed-out shadow. Hume's *Tired*, 1997, is just such a trace, an outline as poignant as an empty bottle. Jasper Johns did something like this too, when he put his outlined figure in his paintings of the *Seasons*, 1985-86, quoting Picasso's earlier insertion of his shadow in the painting *The Studio*, 1928-29.

A new series of very large paintings, which Hume is in the process of completing as I write, have been given the generic title *Water*. The paintings depict fragments of female bodies simply delineated, their outline comprised of heads, breasts, eyes, arms and hands. The figure is endlessly returning to the plane on which it is painted, but

Gary Hume
Tired, 1997
gloss paint on aluminium panel
208 × 117 cm
Collection of Vicki and Kent Logan,
fractional and promised gift to the
permanent collection of the San Francisco
Museum of Modern Art

never returning to the same place twice. These women are there and
they are not there: they slip away and then return. I follow the line
which describes them and divides them from themselves, the line
which draws and redraws their contours across the painting, which
describes too many breasts, a nipple half obscuring a second nipple,
too many heads or the same head too many times. One is bound to
think of Picabia, and his transparent overlaid images, but his was
a more disruptive simultaneity, which played on our inability to
read two things at once. Picabia's paintings depended on a notion of
a consistent pictorial space which was itself transparent, whereas
Hume's fragmented figures are always in the same plane, compressed
into the surface of the painting. Everything is surface, and my
reflection is in there with it as I move around, putting me in the
picture along with the daylight and the shadows in the room where
the painting hangs. The painting doesn't depict movement, but
makes me aware of my own mobile eye, my own body in front of the
painting. Hume plays games with our desire to see and be seen, to
look and be looked at.

The painter's subjects live on the surface. If they have an inner life, a life beyond the painting, it is unknowable. They are floating between us and something unknown. Limpid, fragmentary and weightless, their elusive presences aren't so much watery refractions as the delineations of multiple tracings, repeated glances and endless touches. The drawing dances and drifts, turns on itself, like a thought turned over in the mind, an image recalled for the pleasure of remembering it. These are paintings of great intimacy and strangeness; they pleasure the imagination, as much by what is left out or withheld as by what is described. We invent their fullness, both as forms and as beings. In these paintings the surface has become a screen on which the mind projects its own memories of bodies, its own erotics. Looking at them, these paintings make me feel weightless, as though I were only an eye adrift, floating in an imaginary, intangible mental space.

When I think of Gary Hume painting, I think of his shadow in his daylight studio, crossing and recrossing the painting, along with all the reflections and slicks of light blooming and glaring on the surface. I think of him losing and re-finding himself in the surface, along with the line he is painting. I also think of him drawing-up the picture, at night, moving around between the projector and the painting. His shadow is cast onto the painting, and the projected image is also cast on him. The artist is a screen on which the world is projected, and the painting is another screen, on which the artist projects the world. I wonder why he does not paint himself. But of course he does. He paints himself dissolving in images, losing himself in the painting's surface, finding himself in the things he paints. He is there in the anonymity of the surface, in the strange moments he depicts.

Adrian Searle

OF CANS, CORRUPTION, AND COLOUR

I knew a wise-guy who used to make fun of my painting, but he didn't like the Abstract Expressionists either. He said they would be good painters if they could only keep the paint as good as it is in the can. And that's what I tried to do. I tried to keep the paint as good as it was in the can.

FRANK STELLA, 1964

'To keep the paint as good as it was in the can.' It's a simple enough phrase on the face of it: direct, unambiguous, deadpan, and not unlike Stella's paintings themselves of the time. But it's also a phrase which, behind its flat tones, still carries a kind of resonance. It acknowledges that something important has changed in art. And, as it does so, it also betrays a kind of anxiety. The change in art it acknowledges may not seem so big: it says that paint now comes from a can. That is, from a can rather than from a tube: whereas artists' paints usually come in tubes, industrial or household paints are normally stored in cans. Artists' paints were developed to allow the representation of various kinds of bodies in different types of space. "Flesh was the reason oil painting was invented" said DeKooning. Industrial paints are made to cover large surfaces in a uniform layer of flat colour. They form a skin but they do not suggest flesh. They are for paint-jobs more than for painting-proper. Different technologies which are harnessed to different worlds: in short to use paint from a can rather than from a tube may not seem much, but it carries with it the risk – or the promise – of abandoning the entire tradition of easel painting, of painting as representation. If this idea, and this risk, was hinted at in Europe with Dada and Constructivism, it was again taken up after the war by Pollock, and in the early 1950s by Rauschenberg. By the time Stella had said his piece, a generation of artists was trying out a range of more-or-less recently developed industrial paints, finishes, supports and other materials.

Not only does this paint come in a can, it looks *good* in the can.

The anxiety that Stella's remark betrays does not, or at least does not directly concern the loss of three or more centuries of oil and easel painting. Rather he points in another direction. His concern is not how his work will measure up to the past of art but how it will compare with the paint in the can. Stella says he 'tried to keep it as good as it was in the can'. He 'tried'. . . but he knew he might not succeed. And if he didn't keep it as good . . . so what? What was at stake? Again, it may not sound like much, but in a way it was perhaps almost everything that mattered at the time. Twenty years earlier it couldn't have been said – or at least it wouldn't have meant anything very much. But by the early 1960s Stella's concern had come to stand for something quite critical in the relationship of art with the wider world in which it was situated. That Stella sought to 'keep' the paint that good suggests that he knew it might be hard to improve on the materials in their raw state; that once the paint had been put to use in art it might well be less interesting than when it was 'in the can'. This is the anxiety he describes: the anxiety that the materials of the modern world might be more interesting than anything that can be done with them in a studio. It is an entirely modern anxiety. It is, perhaps, also an unforeseen consequence of the nineteenth century project to paint the dramas and details of modern life – from its billowing chimneys down to its shiny patent leather shoes. It's an anxiety which has continued to haunt artists ever since. But it is also a promise.

Much painting since the 1960s is related in its evasion of oil paint, and, more to the point, in its evasion of the protocols and procedures, the conventions and habits of thought, the training and techniques and tools, the expectations and effects, the surfaces and smells that went with it. Why? What motivated this turn by artists against a technology which had been developed, over three hundred years or so, exclusively for the use of artists? There may be any number of answers to this question. There is an argument – one which was very prominent around the time of Stella's remark – that in order to survive, continue and develop, painting has to distinguish itself from all the other arts and equally from all that is not art.

The artist's studio, 1999

But the evidence of many artists' work at the time and since suggests something like the opposite has turned out to be true. That is, painting has been continued by constantly being tested against that which stands outside painting-as-art: the photograph, the written word, decoration, literalness or objecthood. In other words, painting has been continued by being continuously corrupted; by being made impure rather than pure; by being made ambiguous, uncertain and unstable; and by not limiting itself to its own competences. Painting has been kept going by embracing rather than resisting that which might extinguish it, and this has included embracing the possibility of painting becoming all but indistinguishable from a paint-job. It has also included the possibility of paintings becoming all but indistinguishable from objects, photographs, texts and so forth. But while painting has shown itself to be capable of absorbing these things, it is always equally possible that painting itself might be absorbed *by* them. That is to say, it is a story of the corruption of painting as the continuation of painting; but one which has no guarantee of a happy end, because the corruption of painting must also contain the real possibility of the cancellation of painting. It is a story of the continuation of painting by the corruption of painting, and paint itself is one of the characters in the story. Perhaps one of the differences between a painting and something merely painted is − or, for a while, was − the difference between types of paint. Perhaps artists' colours and materials were art's guarantee, a kind of certainty; art's pedigree in a universe of aliens and impostors and mongrels; its received pronunciation in a world of strange and irregular voices. Perhaps this was the attraction of commercial paints: they seemed also to contain the possibility for both the continuation and the cancellation of painting. And perhaps that is why they looked so good in the can.

Gary Hume's first exhibited paintings appear to take this state of affairs as a point of departure. Household paints, gloss surfaces, uniform colours, flat finishes. At least as much a paint-job as painting-proper. And the imagery: doors: one-to-one scale, no reduction, no perspective, no space, no depth, no atmosphere. Paintings which were less like images of doors than simply door-like. Occasional ridges − regular, measured, symmetrical − mark the main panels and apertures of these typically institutional and functional structures. These were in a way shaped canvases; it's just that the shapes were rectangular. To begin with it must have looked like there wasn't much room to move within the constraints of the *Door Paintings*. It might have appeared that these were sardonic end-of-painting paintings; paintings which acknowledged that the game was up; paint-job paintings which saw that painting was out of a job. But

Gary Hume
Four Subtle Doors, 1989-90
gloss paint on four canvases
238.7 × 594.4 cm
The Saatchi Gallery, London

the fact that Hume *continued* with these works suggests that the
motivation was rather different. Gerhard Richter once described his
Grey Paintings of the mid-sixties as works which were begun in the
belief that painting was no longer capable of renewing itself. But
he went on to say that the results showed him that there was still
room for differentiation, that there was something there other than
empty repetition, that there could still be such a thing as a good
and a bad picture, and that therefore there was still work to do. It is
possible that Hume's *Door Paintings* surprised the artist in a similar
way. The sequence of works seems to suggest that the self-imposed
limitations began, little by little, to reveal a range of possibilities
and unexplored areas where perhaps only repetition had been
imagined. Of these possibilities, one stands out beyond any others:
the possibility of colour.

Colour that comes out of a can is very different from colour that
comes out of a tube. Hume's first *Door Paintings* were magnolia,
a quintessentially institutional colour, a quintessentially non-art
colour. More than that magnolia is an entirely unemphatic colour;
its job is to cover a surface without drawing attention to itself; the
principal quality of this colour is its invisibility; it is a colour which
was designed to be not-seen. Thus a painting of this kind in this
colour might be understood as a painting designed to be not-seen.
Alternatively it might be understood as a painting which begins to
draw attention to the not-seen in the visible world.

A not-seen colour such as magnolia is still a colour, but it is a
paint-job colour rather than a painting colour. Sooner or later
a painter who uses commercial or industrial paints is bound to notice
the vast range of other colours which are on offer at the touch of
a button – there are about two thousand available in the standard
computerised mixing systems. At the heart of this system – although
in an important sense this is an entirely heartless system – lies a

Gary Hume
Four Doors I, 1989-90
gloss paint on four canvases
239 × 594 cm
The Saatchi Gallery, London

The artist's studio, 1999

small strip of paper with a few rectangular swatches of colour printed on it: the colour chart. The colour chart: a disposable list of ready-made colour. Each strip of paper a perfect abstract painting in miniature; or a compact example of colour serialism; or one page of a vast *catalogue raisonné* of monochromes. The colour chart is to commercial colours what the colour circle is to artists' colours. Artists' colours are connected to the palette; the palette is connected to colour mixture; colour mixture is connected to colour theory; colour theory is connected to the colour circle. The colour circle has dominated the understanding and the use of colour in art. Based on a geometry of triangulation and a grammar of complementarity, the colour circle establishes relationships between colours, and also implies an almost feudal hierarchy among colours – primaries, secondaries and tertiaries; the pure and the less pure. The colour chart offers an escape from all that. It is, in effect, simply a list; a grammarless accumulation of discrete colour units. In the colour chart, every colour is equivalent to and independent of every other colour. There are no hierarchies, only isolated colour events. The colour chart divorces colour from conventional colour theory and turns every colour into a readymade. It promises autonomy for colour; in fact it offers three distinct but related types of autonomy: the autonomy of each colour from every other colour, the autonomy of colour from the dictates of colour theory, and the autonomy of colour from the register of representation.

From 1989 Hume's *Door Paintings* are increasingly marked by the availability and the autonomy of the colour chart. The rudimentary geometry of the image provided an opportunity to combine two or three different colours within the same painting, and this was further complicated by the occasional grouping of four paintings to make a single large irregular-shaped work. The colours of these works became increasingly disconnected from the motif-less neutral, less

25

conventional, more intense, more striking, more colours-in-themselves than the colours of painted doors – but their relentlessly flat and glossy finish still held them within the orbit of the door-like.

Flat and glossy: this is one of the paradoxical attractions of commercial paints: the double quality of the dead and the dynamic, the bland and the brilliant. A shiny surface gives depth to flatness at the same time as it emphasises that flatness. But it is a kind of depth which is entirely the opposite of the atmospheric depth of traditional easel painting. This is an inexpressive, mechanical depth. It is not psychological or emotional, at least not in the traditional sense. It reflects not an imaginary inner world but an actual external space: the contingencies of the environment in which the work is situated: the viewer's space. But it is vivid, nonetheless. It is sharp and hard and live, in a vulgar kind of way, and its vulgar sharpness is a part of its attraction.

Flat and glossy and even and bounded: the colour chart colours contribute to a further change in the use and understanding of colour. This might be called the digitalisation of colour, and its opposite is analogical colour. The colour circle is analogical, the colour chart is digital. Analogical colour is a continuum, a seamless spectrum, an undivided whole, a merging of one colour into another. Digital colour is individuated, it comes in discrete units, there is no mergence or modulation, there are only boundaries, steps and edges. The postwar period is the period of the digitalisation of colour in painting. Rauschenberg's monochromes, Warhol's screen prints, Richter's colour chart paintings, Halley's cells and conduits: these all in different ways participate in this process. Even painters who continued to use artists' colours – such as Noland or Kelly – still participate in the differentiation of colour, although there are, of course, many important exceptions. It is not that digital colour is more true than analogical colour. But it may be true that digitalised colours have a stronger relationship with works of art that refer, directly or indirectly, to the experience of modernity. These colours are more the colours of things than atmospheres. More urban colours than the colours of nature. City colours. Industrial colours. Coloured plastics, coloured metals, coloured lights. Local, contingent, materially and culturally specific colours. Colours that are consistent with the images and the materials and the forms of an urban, industrial art.

It is the quality of the colour chart colours and finishes, as much as the quality of the images, which gives Hume's work its particular character. When Hume abandoned the *Door Paintings*, their place was taken – to many people's surprise – by images of figures and flowers and spaces of one kind or another. But the real surprise, perhaps, is that the characteristic mood of the work has remained

Gary Hume
Vicious, 1994
gloss paint on MDF panel
218 × 180 cm
The Saatchi Gallery, London

consistent and in some ways intensified. This is because Hume's
technique has remained more or less consistent. There are figures and
spaces in these pictures but there is very little in the way of a figure-
ground relationship, even in the more recent and relatively detailed
works. The flatness, the shininess, the often edgy and unorthodox
combinations of commercial colours makes for paintings which
are still in some respects door-like even when they depict particular
individuals. For the most part these images are reduced to a few
irregular silhouettes and schematic shapes. The colours remain
entirely autonomous from the image: there is no naturalism, different
parts of one body are often coloured differently, and 'ground' is
given the same weight and intensity as 'figure'. Appropriated images
of Tony Blackburn or Francis Bacon or Kate Moss are, in part,
opportunities to colour-in more irregular shapes in a more informal
and varied way. (They are also, in part, something else entirely: a
door-like image of an individual is bound to be very different from
a door-like image of a door. But that is another story...)

So how are the colours selected, given the absence of any

correspondence between colour and image? One answer would be: independently. Hume's studio contains a number of colour charts and books on colour. Some of these books are strange – like the one picked up in a car boot sale on the proper colours for Empire interiors – but few are volumes of what you would call 'colour theory'. Even if they do contain colour theories, they are not kept for that reason. Rather these charts and books provide suggestions for colours and clusters of colour which are taken entirely and blatantly out of context. On other occasions colour choices have been prompted by observations made outside the studio. One group of paintings made in New York was based on the colours of sweets Hume had seen in shops. The colours of the 1994 painting *Vicious* were derived from colours of a packet of *Refreshers*. There is something very pleasurable, gleeful even, in selecting colours in this way. There is also something deadly serious in this kind of playful appropriation: a recognition of the enormous complexity of colour, and equally a recognition of the sheer contingency of most colour choices. The act of appropriating colours is a means of resisting colour theory; at the same time it is also a means of remaining open to the pleasures of glimpsed colour and colour clusters.

Colour is uncontainable. It effortlessly reveals the limits of language and evades our best attempts to impose a rational order upon it. Colour also reveals more about culture than we might expect or want it to. To work with colour is to become acutely aware of the insufficiency of language and theory – which is both disturbing and pleasurable – and equally aware of the physical and political place of colour in our environments. It is, for example, no accident that Hume was attracted to the colours of bags of sweets. This is one of the places of colour in the West: it is habitually reduced to the realm of the infantile. Or it is feminine, or kitsch, or oriental. That is, not rational, not masculine, not intellectual, not linguistic, not Western. To put colour – and colours: big, bright, intense, commercial colours – at the centre of one's work, even when that work is making paintings, is still a fairly strange thing to do, at least in this country. It involves returning to a culture that which it routinely and often unconsciously excludes, reminding a culture of that which it would rather pass over in silence. And so much the better when there is no excuse for colour – that is, when the motivation is the pleasure of colour itself rather than the demands of representation or the false symmetry of theory.

David Batchelor

PLATES

WATER PAINTING, 1999

WATER PAINTING, 1999

WATER PAINTING, 1999

WATER PAINTING, 1999

RED ANGELS, 1998

YELLOW ANGELS, 1999

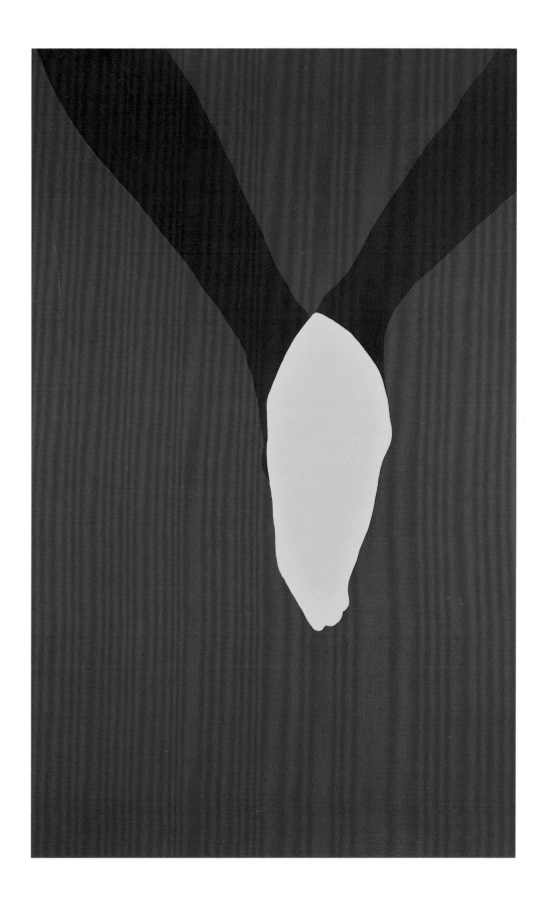

FALLING, 1995

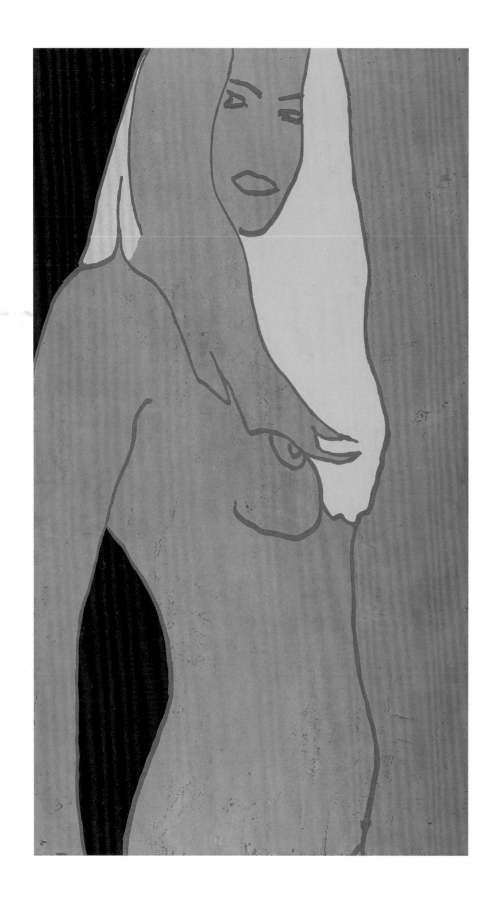

CAVE PAULINE, 1998

PAULINE, 1996

BIRDSONG, 1998

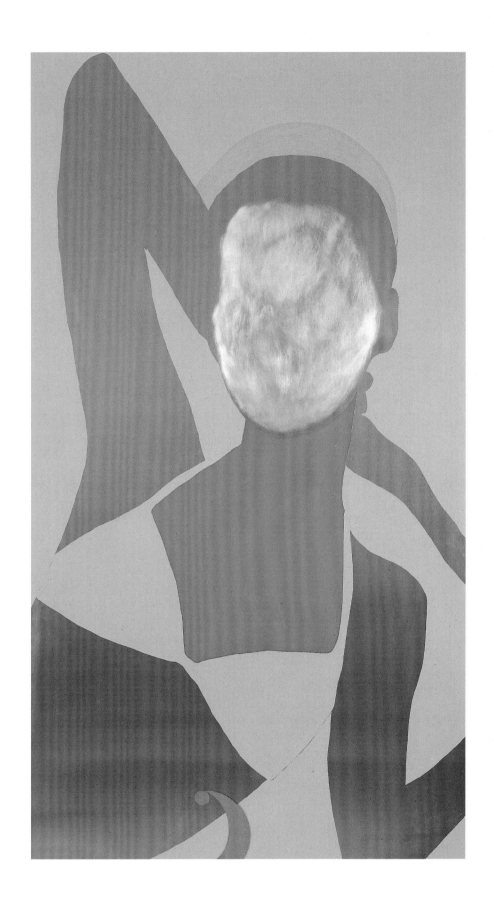

KATE, 1996

WIDOW, 1997

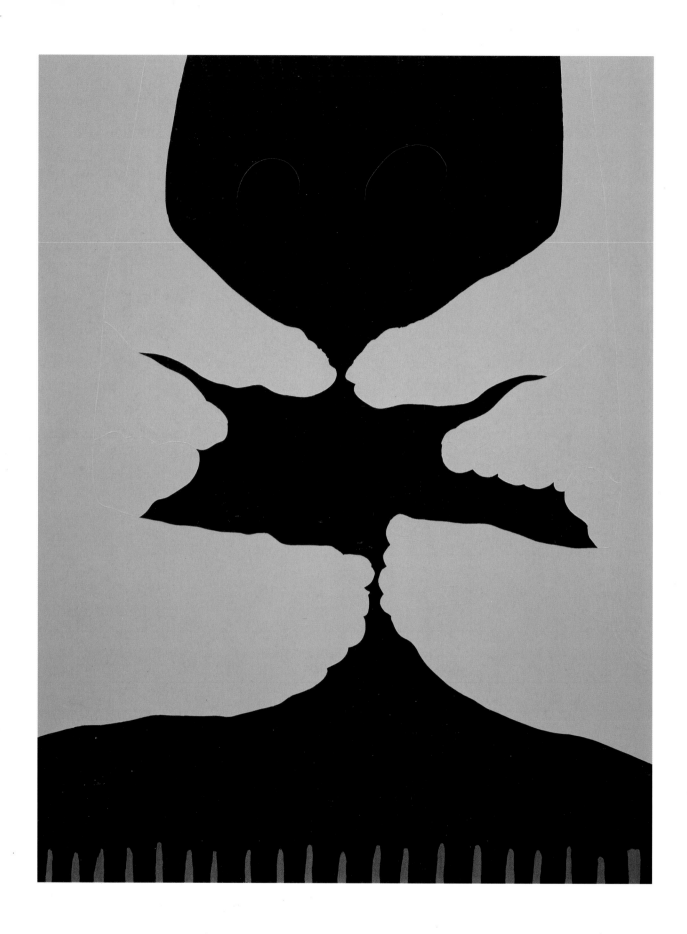

FOUR FEET IN THE GARDEN, 1995

BLACKBIRD, 1998

GARDEN PAINTING NO.1, 1996

YELLOW HAIR, 1995

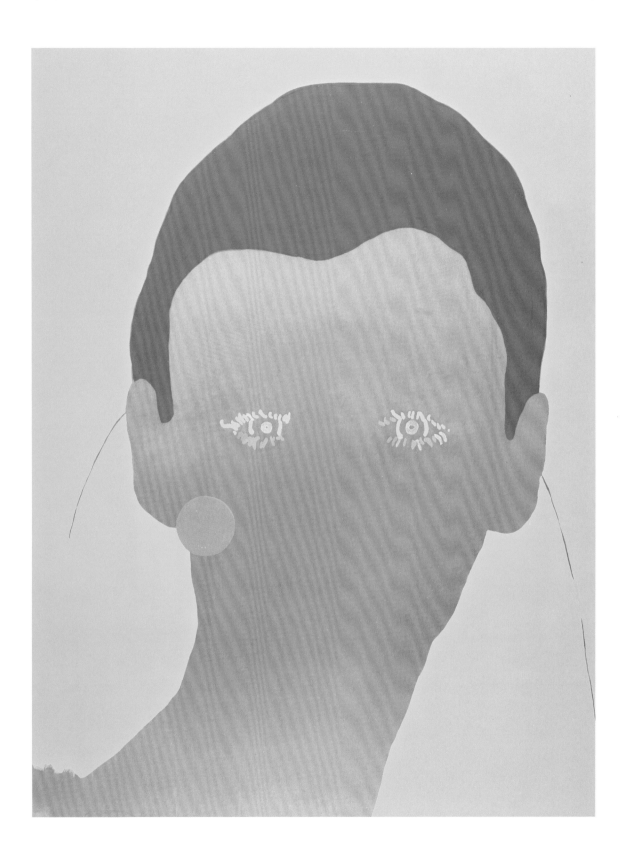

CERITH, 1997

FRANCIS, 1997

FUNNY GIRL, 1995

SCARED, 1999

NEST I, 1998

NEST II, 1998

NEST III, 1998

BIRD ON A BRANCH, 1998

MESSIAH, 1998

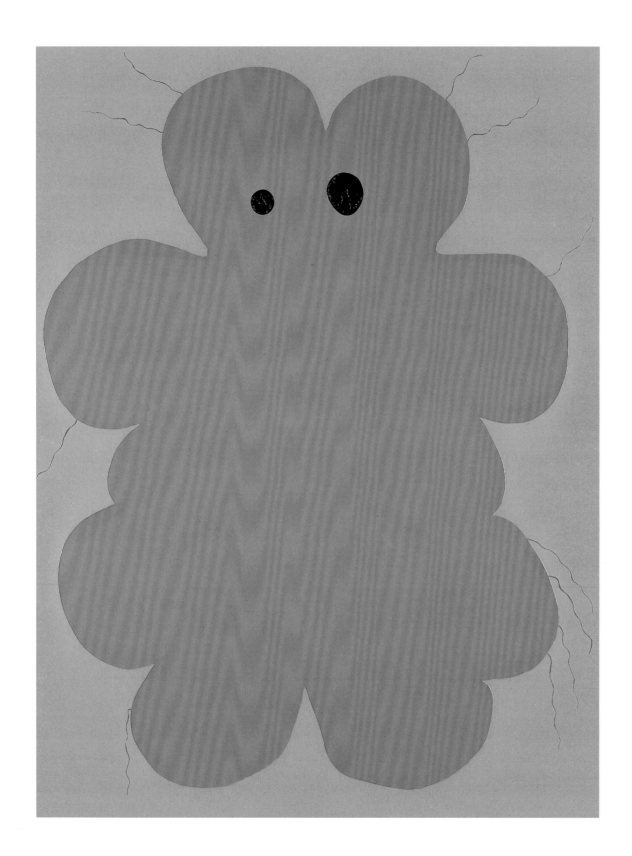

POLAR BEAR, 1994

SNOWMAN, 1996

GARDEN PAINTING NO. 3, 1996

POOR THING, 1994

LADY PARKER (AFTER HOLBEIN), 1998

Magnolia Door VI, VII and IX, 1989, gloss paint on canvas, each 254 × 162.5 cm. Installation view, *Gary Hume: Recent Works*, Karsten Schubert Ltd., London, 1989

Four Subtle Doors, 1989-90, gloss paint on four canvases, 238.7 × 594.4 cm

BIOGRAPHY

1962   Born Kent, England
1988   Graduated, Goldsmiths College,
        University of London
1996   Shortlisted for the Turner Prize,
        Tate Gallery, London
1997   Awarded Jerwood Painting Prize,
        Jerwood Foundation, London

        Lives and works in London

SOLO EXHIBITIONS

1989   *Gary Hume: Recent Works*, Karsten Schubert Ltd.,
        London
1991   *The Dolphin Paintings*, Karsten Schubert Ltd.,
        London
        Tarpaulins, Galerie Tanja Grünert, Cologne
1992   *Recent Paintings*, Matthew Marks Gallery,
        New York
        Recent Paintings, Daniel Weinburg Gallery,
        Santa Monica
1993   Exhibited one new painting, *Madonna & Child*,
        1993, Sarah Lucas' bedsit, Holloway Road, London
        Gary Hume: New Works, Galerie Tanja Grünert,
        Cologne
1994   *Gary Hume*, Matthew Marks Gallery, New York
1995   *Gary Hume*, Jay Jopling/White Cube, London
        Gary Hume, Kunsthalle Berne; Institute of
        Contemporary Art, London; Spacex Gallery, Exeter
        My Aunt and I Agree, Habitat, Kings Road,
        London

1996   *Gary Hume: Garden*, Galerie Gebauer and
        Thumm, Berlin
        Gary Hume, Galleria il Ponte, Rome, solo
        exhibition under the auspices of *Artisti britannica
        a Roma*, organised by Mario Codognato and the
        British Council
        Gary Hume, Bonnefantenmuseum, Maastricht
        Gary Hume, XXIII Bienal de São Paulo
1997   *Gary Hume*, Matthew Marks Gallery, New York
1998   *Gary Hume: Night-time Window Projections*, LEA
        Gallery, London
        Gary Hume: Small Paintings, Matthew Marks
        Gallery, New York
        Turnaround: Inside Out at the Hayward, Hayward
        Gallery, London
        Gary Hume, Sadler's Wells Theatre, London
1999   *Gary Hume*, British Pavilion, XLVIII Venice
        Biennale of Art
        Gary Hume, Scottish National Gallery of Modern
        Art, Edinburgh
        Gary Hume, Whitechapel Art Gallery, London

GROUP EXHIBITIONS

1988   *Freeze Part II*, Surrey Docks, London. Curated by
        Damien Hirst.
        Ian Davenport, Gary Hume, Michael Landy,
        Karsten Schubert Ltd., London
1989   *Steve DiBenedetto, Gary Hume, Julian Lethbridge,
        Nicholas Rule, Matthew Weinstein*, Lorence Monk

Four Doors I, 1989-90, gloss paint on four canvases, 239 × 594 cm

Four Doors II, 1990, gloss paint on four canvases, 213.4 × 589.3 cm

Gallery, New York. Curated by Clarissa Dalrymple.
Angela Bulloch, Gary Hume, Michael Landy,
Esther Schipper, Cologne

1990 *A Paintings Show: Michael Craig-Martin, Gary*
Hume, Christopher Wood, Karsten Schubert Ltd.,
London
The British Art Show 1990, touring exhibition
organised by the Hayward Gallery, for the
Arts Council of England
The Köln Show, Galerie Jablonka, Cologne
East Country Yard Show, East Country Yard,
London. Curated by Henry Bond & Sarah Lucas.

1991 *Drawings: Hanne Darboven, Gary Hume, Bob Law,*
Julian Lethbridge, Karsten Schubert Ltd., London
Artists' Sketchbooks, Matthew Marks Gallery,
New York
Summer Group Exhibition, Matthew Marks Gallery,
New York
Paintings & Drawings, Daniel Weinberg Gallery,
Santa Monica
Broken English: Angela Bulloch, Ian Davenport,
Anya Gallaccio, Damien Hirst, Gary Hume,
Michael Landy, Sarah Staton, Rachel Whiteread,
Serpentine Gallery, London. Curated by Andrew
Graham-Dixon, Julia Peyton-Jones & Andrea
Schlieker.
Act-Up Benefit Exhibition, Paula Cooper Gallery,
New York
Confrontaciones: Arte último británico y español,
Museo Nacional Centro de Arte Reina Sofía, Madrid,
organised in collaboration with the British Council

1992 *5th Anniversary Exhibition,* Karsten Schubert Ltd.,
London
Etats spécifiques, Musée des Beaux-Arts André
Malraux, Le Havre
Nayland Blake, Richmond Burton, Peter Cain,
Gary Hume, Matthew Marks Gallery, New York
Summer Group Show: Keith Coventry, Gary Hume,
Michael Landy, Bridget Riley, Rachel Whiteread,
Alison Wilding, Karsten Schubert Ltd., London
Lea Andrews, Keith Coventry, Anya Gallaccio,
Damien Hirst, Gary Hume, Abigail Lane, Sarah
Lucas, Steven Pippin, Marc Quinn, Marcus Taylor,
Rachel Whiteread, Barbara Gladstone Gallery,
New York. Curated by Clarissa Dalrymple.
New Voices: New works for the British Council
Collection, international touring exhibition
organised by the British Council
Group Exhibition, Galerie Tanja Grünert, Cologne
Il Mistero dei 100 Dollari Scomparsi, Gio' Marconi
Gallery, Milan

1993 *The Rome Project,* David Winton Bell Gallery,
List Art Center, Brown University, Providence,
Rhode Island
Launch, Curtain Road Arts, London. Produced by
Angela Daniel. First showing of *King Cnut* video,
1993.
Spit in the Ocean: Gerald Hemsworth, Gary Hume,
Mark Wallinger, Anthony Reynolds Gallery,
London
Wonderful Life, Lisson Gallery, London
A Fête Worse Than Death, Charlotte Road and

Four Subtle Doors II, 1989-90, gloss paint on four canvases, 213.4 × 589.3 cm

Four Coloured Doors, 1990, gloss paint on four MDF panels, 213.4 × 589.3 cm

Rivington Street, London. Organised by Joshua Compston/Factual Nonsense.
Lucky Kunst, Part I, 2 Silver Place, London & *Close Up*, Part II, 233 West 42nd Street, New York. Co-ordinated by Ricardo De Oliveira, Sarah Morris and Gregor Muir.
Close Up, Times Square, New York

1994 *Unbound: Possibilities in Painting*, Hayward Gallery, London. Curated by Greg Hilty and Adrian Searle.
The Magic Touch; New works by Gary Hume, Mark Wigan & PPQ, 30 Redchurch Street, London
Not Self Portrait, Karsten Schubert Ltd., London
Football Karaoke, Portikus, Frankfurt

1995 *Gary Hume, Udomsak Krisanamis, Rirkrit Tiravanija*, Gavin Brown's Enterprise, New York
From Here, Waddington Galleries/Karsten Schubert Gallery, London
Minky Manky, South London Gallery, London; Arnolfini, Bristol. Curated by Carl Freedman.
General Release: Young British Artists at Scuola di San Pasquale, organised by the British Council, XLV1 Venice Biennale
The Hanging Picnic, Hoxton Square, London. Organised by Joshua Compston/Factual Nonsense.
Wild Walls, Stedelijk Museum, Amsterdam
Other Men's Flowers, Icebox, Athens. Print portfolio, selected by Joshua Compston, published by The Paragon Press. Subsequently shown at Aurel Scheibler, Cologne; The British School at Rome and the Irish Museum of Modern Art, Dublin.

Brilliant! New Art from London, Walker Art Center, Center, Minneapolis; Contemporary Arts Museum, Houston
Hardcore (Part II), Factual Nonsense, London
The British Art Show 4, National Touring Exhibition, organised by the Hayward Gallery for the Arts Council of England

1996 *Ace! Arts Council Collection: New Purchases*, National Touring Exhibition, organised by the Hayward Gallery for the Arts Council of England
Intermission, Basilico Fine Art, New York
A Small Shifting Sphere of Serious Culture, ICA, London. Part of Pandemonium I, single screen works, Festival of Moving Images. Curated by Gregor Muir.
Such is Life, video programme, Serpentine Gallery Bookshop, London; Palais des Beaux Arts, Brussels. Curated by Jonathan Watkins.
The Turner Prize 1996, Tate Gallery, London
About Vision: New British Painting in the 1990s, Museum of Modern Art, Oxford
Full House: Young British Art, Kunstmuseum Wolfsburg, Wolfsburg

1997 *Fiona Rae, Gary Hume*, The Saatchi Gallery, London
A Ilha do Tesouro/Treasure Island, Centro de Arte Moderna José de Azeredo Perdigão, Fundação Calouste Gulbenkian, Lisbon
Renovate, Shoreditch Town Hall, London. Co-ordinated by Monica Chung and Alice Sharp.
Multiple Choice: Obras impesad de jovens artistas

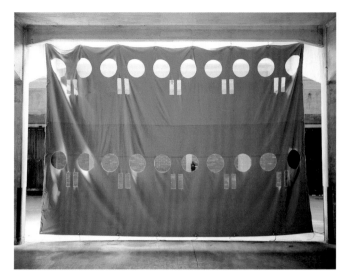

Bay A – Bay K, 1990, Tarpaulins
Installation view, *East Country Yard Show*, London, 1990

Bay C, 1990, Tarpaulin, 442 × 635 cm
Installation view, *East Country Yard Show*, London, 1990

Británicos, international touring exhibition organised by the British Council
Truce: Echoes of Art in an Age of Endless Conclusions, Site Santa Fe, New Mexico. Curated by Francesco Bonami.
Package Holiday, Hydra Workshops, Hydra, Greece. Curated by Sadie Coles.
Display, Charlottenborg Museum of Contemporary Art, Copenhagen
Sensation: Young British Artists from the Saatchi Collection, Royal Academy of Arts, London; Hamburger Bahnhof, Berlin
Jerwood Painting Prize 1997, Lethaby Galleries, Central St Martins College of Art & Design, London
Dimensions Variable, international touring exhibition organised by the British Council

1998 *The Janet Wolfson de Botton Gift*, Tate Gallery, London
The Sound of One Hand: the collection of Collier Schorr, Apex Art, New York
Tuning Up, No. 5, Kunstmuseum Wolfsburg, Wolfsburg
Real/Life: New British Art, Japanese touring exhibition organised by Asahi Shimbun and the British Council
The Summer Exhibition, Royal Academy of Arts, London
London Calling, The British School at Rome, Rome
UK: Maximum Diversity, Gallery Krinzinger at

Benger Fabrik Bregenz, Austria; Atelierhaus der Akademie der Bildenden Künste Wien, Vienna
Distinctive Elements: Contemporary British Art, National Museum of Contemporary Art, Seoul, organised in conjunction with the British Council
Richard Wentworth's Thinking Aloud, a National Touring Exhibition organised by the Hayward Gallery, for the Arts Council of England. Curated by Richard Wentworth.
The Enchanted Garden, Victoria Pleasure Gardens, Shaftesbury, Dorset

1999 *Signature Press: Contemporary British Prints and Multiples*, Alan Cristea Gallery, London
Hirst, Fairhurst, Hume, Coventry, Quinn, Helly Nahmad Gallery, London
Graphics! British Prints Now, Yale Center for British Art, New Haven, Connecticut

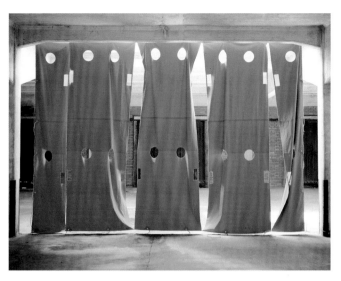

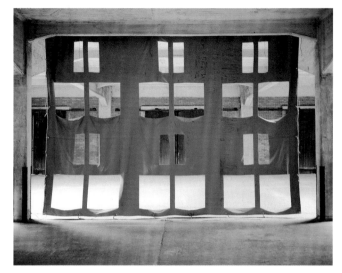

Bay H, 1990, Tarpaulin, 442 × 635 cm
Installation view, *East Country Yard Show*, London, 1990

Bay I, 1990, Tarpaulin, 442 × 635 cm
Installation view, *East Country Yard Show*, London, 1990

SOLO EXHIBITION CATALOGUES

1995 *Gary Hume Paintings*, Kunsthalle Berne/Institute of Contemporary Arts, London. Texts by Ulrich Loock & Gregor Muir. English/German.

1996 *Gary Hume*, Bonnefantenmuseum, Maastricht. Text by Francesco Bonami.
Gary Hume: Floor to Ceiling, The British Council, London. Pop-up model of installation, produced on the occasion of the XXIII São Paulo Bienal, with text by Caroline Douglas. English & Portuguese editions.

GROUP EXHIBITION CATALOGUES

1988 *Freeze*, London. Text by Ian Jeffrey.

1990 *The British Art Show 1990*, The South Bank Centre, London. Texts by Caroline Collier, Andrew Nairne & David Ward.
East Country Yard Show, London.
A paintings show: Michael Craig-Martin, Gary Hume, Christopher Wool, Karsten Schubert Ltd., London. Text by Lynne Cooke.
Supply: The Köln Show, Cologne. Edited by Isabelle Graw. Texts by Fareed Armaly, Cosima von Bonin, Deidrich Deiderichten, Michaela Eichwald, Andrea Fraser, Isabelle Graw, Kay Heymer, Jutta Koether, Johannes Meinhardt, John Miller, Silke Panse, Mark Sikora, Mayo Thompson & Gunnar Wardenbach. English/German.

1991 *Artists Sketchbooks*, Matthew Marks Gallery, New York. Text by Guy Davenport.
Broken English: Angela Bulloch, Ian Davenport,
Anya Gallaccio, Damien Hirst, Gary Hume, Michael Landy, Sarah Staton, Rachel Whiteread, Serpentine Gallery, London. Text by Andrew Graham-Dixon.
Confrontaciones: Arte último británico y español, Instituto de la Juventud, Madrid. Texts by Teresa Blanch, Félix Guisasola & Andrew Renton. English/Spanish.

1992 *Etats spécifiques*, Musée des Beaux-Arts André Malraux, Le Havre. Texts by Michael Archer & Françoise Cohen. English/French.
Il Mistero dei 100 Dollari Scomparsi, Gio' Marconi Gallery, Milan. Text by Liam Gillick. English/Italian.
Lea Andrews, Keith Coventry, Anya Gallaccio, Damien Hirst, Gary Hume, Abigail Lane, Sarah Lucas, Steven Pippin, Marc Quinn, Marcus Taylor, Rachel Whiteread, Barbara Gladstone/Stein Gladstone. Text by Liam Gillick. Artist's book published to coincide with exhibition at Barbara Gladstone Gallery, New York.
New Voices: New works for the British Council Collection, The British Council, London. Text by Gill Hedley.

1993 *The Rome Project*, Brown University, Providence, Barbara Gladstone and Thea Westreich, New York. Texts by Barbara Gladstone, Thea Westreich & Diana L. Johnson.

1994 *The Magic Touch: New works by Gary Hume, Mark Wigan and PPQ*, PPQ, London. 6 page A4 leaflet to accompany exhibition.

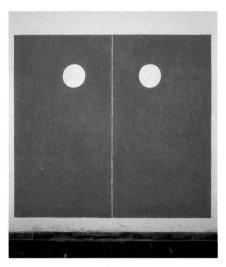

Untitled Wall Painting, 1990, whitewash
and pigment, 179.5 × 198 cm

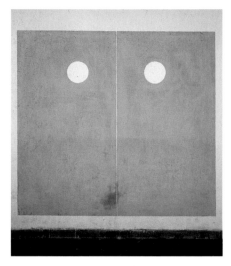

Untitled Wall Painting, 1990, whitewash
and pigment, 179.5 × 198 cm

Unbound: Possibilities in Painting, The South
Bank Centre, London. Text by Adrian Searle.

1995 *Brilliant! New Art from London*, Walker Art
Center, Minneapolis. Texts by Richard Flood,
Douglas Fogle, Stuart Morgan & Neville Wakefield.
Interviews with artists by Douglas Fogle & Marcelo
Spinelli.
The British Art Show 4, National Touring Exhibi-
tions, The South Bank Centre, London. Texts by
Richard Cork, Rose Finn-Kelcey & Thomas Lawson.
From Here, Waddington Galleries/Karsten
Schubert, London. Text by Andrew Wilson.
*General Release: Young British Artists at Scuola di
San Pasquale*, The British Council, London. Edited
by Ann Gallagher & James Roberts. Texts by
Gregor Muir & James Roberts. Art and social
chronology by Gregor Muir, James Roberts &
Clarrie Rudrum.
Minky Manky, South London Art Gallery, London.
Interviews with artists by Carl Freedman.
New Voices, The British Council, London. Text by
Adrian Searle.
Wild Walls, Stedelijk Museum, Amsterdam. Texts
by Leontine Coelewij & Martin van Nieuwenhuyzen.

1996 *XXIII Bienal de São Paulo*, Fundação Bienal de
São Paulo. Text by Simon Bill, p.170.
English/Portuguese.
About Vision: New British Painting in the 1990s,
Museum of Modern Art, Oxford. Text by David
Elliott.
Ace! Arts Council Collection New Purchases,

National Touring Exhibitions, The South Bank
Centre, London. Petit journal with text by Gavin
Robson.
Artisti britannici a Roma, Umberto Allemandi & C.,
Rome. Text by Mario Codognato. English/Italian.
Full House: Young British Art, Kunstmuseum
Wolfsburg, Wolfsburg. Bound reader and folded
A3 poster with text by Veit Görner. German.
The Turner Prize 1996, Tate Gallery Publishing
Ltd., London. Text by Virginia Button.

1997 *Dimensions Variable: New Works for the British
Council Collection*, The British Council, London.
Text by Ann Gallagher.
Display, Charlottenborg Museum of Contemporary
Art, Copenhagen. Text by Michael Anderson.
Danish/English.
Fiona Rae, Gary Hume, The Saatchi Gallery,
London. Text by Sarah Kent.
A Ilha do Tesouro/Treasure Island, Centro de Arte
Moderna José de Azeredo Perdigão, Fundação
Calouste Gulbenkian, Lisbon.
Texts by Jorge Molder, Rui Sanche & Ana de
Vasconcelos e Melo. Interviews with Alan Bowness,
Richard Cork, Gill Hedley, Andrew Renton,
Bryan Robertson & Richard Shone.
English/Portuguese.
Jerwood Painting Prize 1997, Jerwood Foundation,
London. Text by Judith Bumpus.
*Multiple Choice: Obras impesad de jovenes artistas
Britanicos*, The British Council, London. Text by
Sara Roberts. Spanish.

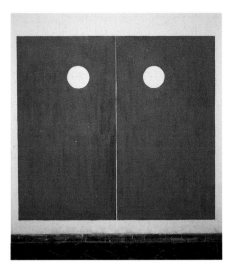

Untitled Wall Painting, 1990, whitewash
and pigment, 179.5 × 198 cm

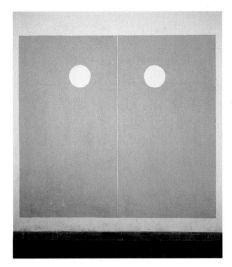

Untitled Wall Painting, 1990, whitewash
and pigment, 179.5 × 198 cm

Package Holiday, Hydra Workshops, Hydra. Text
by Sadie Coles.
*Sensation: Young British Artists from the Saatchi
Collection*, Royal Academy of Arts, London. Texts
by Brooks Adams, Lisa Jardin, Martin Maloney,
Norman Rosenthal & Richard Shone. English &
German editions.
*Truce: Echoes of Art in an Age of Endless
Conclusions*, Site Santa Fe, New Mexico. Edited by
Janine Sieja. Texts by Francesco Bonami, Bobbie
Forshay-Miller, Thomas L. Friedman, Louis
Grachos, John Phillips & Collier Schorr.

1998 *Contemporary Art: The Janet Wolfson de Botton
Gift*, Tate Gallery Publications, London. Edited by
Monique Beudert & Sean Rainbird.
*Distinctive Elements: Contemporary British Art
Exhibition*, National Museum of Contemporary Art,
Seoul. Introduction by Michael Archer & Junmo
Chung. Texts by Michael Archer, Lionel Bovier,
Mario Codognato, Angus Fairhurst, Alex
Farquharson, Charles Harrison, Lee Sook-Kyung,
Simon Morrissey, David Musgrove & John Slyce.
English/Korean.
Real/Life: New British Art, The Asahi Shimbun,
Tokyo. Text by James Roberts in English/
Japanese. Texts by Akio Obigane, Junichi Shioda,
Hiroya Sugimura & James Roberts in Japanese.
Richard Wentworth's Thinking Aloud, National
Touring Exhibition, Hayward Gallery, The South
Bank Centre, London. Text by Nick Groom. Inter-
view with Richard Wentworth by Roger Malbert.

*The Sound of One Hand: the collection of Collier
Schorr*, Apex Art C.P., New York. Leaflet with text
by Collier Schorr.
Tuning Up, No. 5, Kunstmuseum Wolfsburg, Wolfs-
burg. Leaflet with text by Holger Broeker. German.
UK Maximum Diversity, Aterlierhaus der
Akademie der bildenden Künste Wien, Vienna.
Text by Ursula Krinzinger. English.

1999 *Graphics! British Prints Now.* Yale Center for
British Art, New Haven. 12 page A4 brochure with
text by Gillian Forrester.
Hirst, Fairhurst, Hume, Coventry, Quinn. Helly
Nahmad Gallery Ltd., London.
Examining Pictures: exhibiting paintings,
Whitechapel Art Gallery, London.

PERIODICAL AND NEWSPAPER
ARTICLES

1988 Craddock, Sacha. 'Freeze: The fast Dockland train
to simplicity', *The Guardian*, 13 September, p.17.
Review of *Freeze*, London, 1988.

1989 Archer, Michael. 'Ian Davenport, Gary Hume,
Michael Landy', *Artforum*, vol.27, no.6, February,
p.147. Review of group exhibition at Karsten
Schubert Gallery, London, 1988.
Bulloch, Angela. 'Freeze', *Art and Design*, vol.5,
no.3/4, pp.52-53. Article on *Freeze*, London, 1988.
Carpenter, Merlin. 'Gary Hume', *Artscribe*, no.78,
November/December, pp.74-75. Review of first
solo exhibition at Karsten Schubert Gallery,
London, 1989.

Dolphin Painting I, 1990-91, gloss paint on four MDF panels, 218 × 590 cm

Dolphin Painting III, 1991, gloss paint on two MDF panels, 228.5 × 279 cm

Dannatt, Adrian. 'Gary Hume', *Flash Art International*, no.148, October, pp.138-139. Review of group exhibition at Karsten Schubert Gallery, London, 1989.

Kent, Sarah. 'Gary Hume', *Time Out*, no.986, 12-19 July, p.37. Review of first solo exhibition at Karsten Schubert Gallery, London, 1989.

Renton, Andrew. 'Gary Hume', *Blitz Magazine*, no.80, August, p.82.

Roberts, James. 'Gary Hume', *Artefactum*, vol.6, no.31, November/December, p.42. Review of first solo exhibition at Karsten Schubert Gallery, London, 1989.

Shone, Richard. 'Ian Davenport, Gary Hume, Michael Landy', *Burlington Magazine*, vol.121, no.1030, January, p.56. Review of group exhibition at Karsten Schubert Gallery, London, 1989.

1990 Brooks, Liz. 'Spacier and spacier', Artscribe, no.83, September/October, p.16. Review of *East Country Yard Show*, London, 1990.

Collings, Matthew. 'Britain is Best', *Modern Painters*, vol.3, no.1, Spring, pp.90-91. Review of *The British Art Show 1990*.

Gillick, Liam. 'Critical Dementia: The British Art Show', *Art Monthly*, no.134, March, pp.14-16. Review of *The British Art Show 1990*.

Graham-Dixon, Andrew. 'The Midas Touch?: Graduates of Goldsmiths' School of Art dominate the current British art scene', *The Independent*, 31 July, Arts section, p.13.

Graham-Dixon, Andrew. 'Young Turks and Old Masters', *Art News*, vol.89, no.9, November, pp.124-126.

Renton, Andrew. 'Birth of the Cool', *Blitz Magazine*, June, pp.54-56.

Renton, Andrew. 'Disfiguring: Certain New Photographers and Uncertain Images', *Creative Camera*, no.306, October/November, pp.16-45.

Renton, Andrew. 'East Country Yard Show', *Flash Art International*, October, vol.23, no.154, p.191.

White, Tony. 'East Country Yard Show', *Artists Newsletter*, October, pp.37-38.

1991 Collings, Matthew. 'Gary Hume at Karsten Schubert', *City Limits*, no.510, 11 July, p.21. Review of exhibition at Karsten Schubert Gallery, London, 1991.

Collings, Matthew. '*New Contemporaries* at the ICA and *Broken English* at the Serpentine Gallery', *City Limits*, 15-22 August, no.515, p.18.

Francis, Mary Anne. 'London Summer Round Up', *Art Monthly*, no.149, September, pp.24-25. Review of various summer exhibitions in London.

Gale, Iain. 'Broken English', *The Independent*, 13 August, Arts section p.13. Review of *Broken English*, Serpentine Gallery, London, 1991.

Gillick, Liam. 'The Placebo Effect', *Arts Magazine*, vol.65, no.9, May, pp.56-59.

Hall, Charles. 'Tests of Raw Nerves', *The Sunday Times*, 10 August, p.V 10.

Kent, Sarah. 'Breaking Ground', *Time Out*, no.1095, 14-21 August, p.39.

Lillington, David. 'Gary Hume at Karsten

Dolphin Painting IV, 1991, gloss paint on four MDF panels,
222 × 643 cm

Untitled Wall Paintings, 1991, whitewash and pigment,
each 179.5 × 198 cm. Installation view, *Summer Group Exhibition*,
Matthew Marks Gallery, New York, 1991

Schubert', *Time Out*, no.1090, 10-17 July, p.49.
Morgan, Stuart. 'Gary Hume at Karsten Schubert
Ltd', *Artscribe*, no.89, November/December, p.98.
Sewell, Brian. 'Putting on the zits', *Evening
Standard*, 8 August, p.21. Review of *Broken
English*, Serpentine Gallery, London, 1991.

1992   Adams, Brooks. 'Gary Hume', *Art in America*,
vol.80, no.5, May, pp.134-5. Review of exhibition
at Matthew Marks Gallery, New York, 1992.
Ardenne, Paul. 'Onze artistes anglais, Musée des
Beaux-Arts' (Le Havre), *Art Press Magazine*,
no.172, September, p.77. Review of *Etats
spécifiques*, Le Havre, 1992.
Bonami, Francesco. 'Young British Artists', *Flash
Art International*, vol.25, no.167, November, p.87.
Gary Hume at Matthew Marks', *The New Yorker*,
2 March, p.11.
Grout, Catherine. 'Etats Spécifiques', *Artefactum*,
no.45, September/November, p.47. Review of
Etats spécifiques, Le Havre, 1992.
Liebmann, Lisa. 'Gary Hume', *Artforum*, vol.30,
no.8, April, p.94. Review of exhibition at
Matthew Marks Gallery, New York, 1992.
Melrod, George. 'Nayland Blake, Richard Burton,
Peter Cain and Gary Hume at Matthew Marks',
Art News, vol.91, no.9, November, pp.140-142.
Myerson, Clifford. 'On Painting I', *Art Monthly*,
no.179, September, pp.13-15.
Nargi, Lela. 'Ridicule & the '80s: New Works by
John Alexander and Gary Hume', *New York
Perspectives*, 28 February, p.8. Review of exhibition

at Matthew Marks Gallery, New York, 1992.
Schenk-Sorge, Jutta. 'Zwölf Junge Britische
Künstler: Stein Gladstone und Barbara Gladstone
Gallery, New York', *Kunstforum International*,
vol.120, November, pp.397-398. German.
Schjeldhal, Peter. 'Twelve British Artists at
Barbara Gladstone Gallery and Stein Gladstone,
New York', *frieze*, issue 7, December, p.45.
Smith, Roberta. 'A Young Group From Britain',
The New York Times, 16 October.

1993   Searle, Adrian. 'Shut that door', *frieze*, issue 11,
Summer, pp.46-49.

1994   Archer, Michael. 'Unbound', *Art & Text*, no.48,
p.85. Review of *Unbound: Possibilities in Painting*,
Hayward Gallery, London, 1994.
Batchelor, David. 'Behind a painted smile', *frieze*,
issue 16, May/June, pp.18-21, Review of
Unbound: Possibilities in Painting, Hayward
Gallery, London, 1994.
Graham-Dixon, Andrew. 'Sort of, almost, in a way,
nearly', *The Independent*, Tuesday 15 March, p.23.
Review of *Unbound: Possibilities in Painting*,
Hayward Gallery, London, 1994.
Smith, Roberta. 'Gary Hume', *The New York
Times*, 21 October, p.C29. Review of exhibition at
Matthew Marks Gallery, New York, 1994.

1995   Adams, Brooks. 'Gary Hume', *frieze*, issue 20,
January/February, pp.50-51. Review of exhibition
at Matthew Marks Gallery, New York, 1995.
Archer, Michael. 'Home and away', *Art Monthly*,
no.188, July/August, pp.8-10. Review of *General*

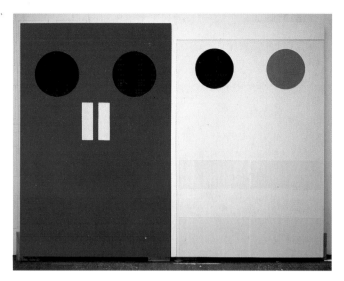

Girl Boy, Boy Girl, 1991, gloss paint on two MDF panels, 208.7 × 282.5 cm

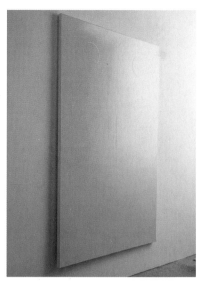

Magnolia Door VI, 1989, gloss paint on canvas, 254 × 162.5 cm

Release: Young British Artists at Scuola di San Pasquale, Venice Biennale, 1995.

Bangma, Anke. 'Wild Walls', *frieze*, issue 25, November/December, pp.61-62. Review of *Wild Walls*, Stedelijk Museum, Amsterdam, 1995.

Bevan, Roger. 'Entrepreneurial, confrontational and working class: it's Brilliant!', *The Art Newspaper*, no.52, October, p.10. Article on *Brilliant!: New Art from London*, Walker Arts Center, Minneapolis, 1995.

Collings, Matthew. 'Welcome to our repartee', *Modern Painters*, vol.8, no.4, Winter, pp.24-28. Review of *Brilliant!: New Art from London*, Walker Arts Center, Minneapolis, 1995.

Cork, Richard. 'Figures add up to newfound freedom', *The Times*, 12 September, p.33a. Review of exhibition at the Institute of Contemporary Arts, London, 1995.

Cork, Richard. 'Hirst among equals', *The Times*, 10 May, p.31a. Review of *Minky Manky*, South London Gallery and solo exhibition at White Cube, May 1995.

Corrigan, Susan. 'Americana', *The Observer*, 12-19 November, p.46. Review of *Brilliant!: New Art from London*, Walker Arts Center, Minneapolis, 1995.

Currah, Mark. 'Beige watch', *Time Out*, no.1308, 13-29 September, p.51. Review of exhibition at the Institute of Contemporary Arts, London, 1995.

Currah, Mark. 'Gary Hume', *Time Out*, no.1289, 3-10 May, p.47. Review of first solo show at White Cube, London, 1995.

Dannatt, Adrian. 'The Luxury of Doing Nothing', *Flash Art International*, no.183, Summer, pp.97-99. Interview with the artist.

'Frieze talks to Richard Flood, curator of 'Brilliant!',' *frieze*, issue 25, November/December, pp.32-36.

Gale, Iain, 'In the realm of the senses', *The Independent*, 28 November, Arts section pp.8-9.

Gale, Iain. 'So slick, so appealing', *The Independent*, 12 September, Arts section p.13. Review of exhibition at the Institute of Contemporary Arts, London, 1995.

Goodman, Jonathan. 'Gary Hume, *Art News*, vol.94, no.1, January, p.164. Review of exhibition at Matthew Marks Gallery, New York, 1995.

Gott, Richard. 'Where the art is', *The Guardian*, 7 October, p.36. Article on London as the new capital of the artworld.

Guha, Tania. 'A gloss on Gary', *Vogue*, April, p.71.

Guha, Tania. 'Hardcore Part 2', *Time Out*, no.1314, 25 October-1 November, p.48. Review of *Hardcore Part 2*, Factual Nonsense, London, 1995.

Hall, James. 'Grime under the Gloss', *The Guardian*, 12 September, p.10. Review of exhibition at the Institute of Contemporary Arts, London, 1995.

Hall, James. 'A smaller splash', *The Guardian*, 11 April, p.4. Review of *From Here*, Waddington Galleries/Karsten Schubert, London, 1995.

Kastner, Jeffrey. 'Brilliant?', *Art Monthly*, no.192, December 1995/ January 1996, pp.10-11, 13-15.

Long Distance Run Around (24 hours), 1991, gloss paint on two formica panels, 218.4 × 365.8 cm

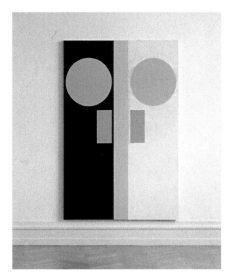

Dream, 1991, gloss paint on formica panel, 208.3 × 139.7 cm

Review of *Brilliant!: New Art from London*, Walker Arts Center, Minneapolis, 1995.

Lillington, David. 'Iconen van vertwijfeling: Een interview met schilder Gary Hume', *Metropolis*, no.3, pp.36-39. Interview with the artist. Dutch.

Lutyens, Dominic. 'Gary Hume', *What's On in London*, 27 September, p.21. Review of exhibition at the Institute of Contemporary Arts, London, 1995.

MacRitchie, Lynn. 'Shock artists', *Financial Times*, 17 November, p.15. Review of *Brilliant!: New Art from London*, Walker Arts Center, Minneapolis, 1995.

Maloney, Martin. 'Gary Hume', *Artforum*, vol.34, no.4, December, pp.62, 65.

Muir, Gregor. 'Vague', *Art & Text*, no.51, May, pp.38-43. Interview with the artist.

Planca, Elisabetta. 'Città d'arte: Londra', *Arte* (Italy), no.266, October 1995, pp.98-105. Italian.

Searle, Adrian. 'Life, the universe and everything', *The Independent*, 18 April, p.20. Review of *Minky Manky*, South London Gallery, 1995.

Smith, Roberta. 'Some British Moderns Seeking to Shock', *The New York Times*, 23 November, pp.C11, C14. Review of *Brilliant!: New Art from London*, Walker Arts Center, Minneapolis, 1995.

Tomkins, Calvin. 'London Calling', *The New Yorker*, 11 December, Review of *Brilliant!: New Art from London*, Walker Arts Center, Minneapolis, 1995.

Wakefield, Neville. 'Gary Hume', *Artforum*, vol.33, no.5, January, pp.84-85. Review of exhibition at

Matthew Marks Gallery, New York, 1995.

Wakefield, Neville. 'Quite Brilliant', *tate: The Art Magazine*, issue 7, Winter, pp.32-39. Re-print of essay for the catalogue of *Brilliant!: New Art from Britain*, Walker Arts Center, Minneapolis, 1995.

Wilson, Andrew. 'Breaking content from form', *Art & Design*, vol.10, March/April, pp.7-19.

Zaugg, Fred. 'Schwingtüren und die Farbe Magnolia', *Der Bund*, 12 May. Review of exhibition at the Kunsthalle Berne. German.

1996   Barbosa, Mariana. 'Gary Hume apresemta obras figurativas', *O Estado de São Paulo* (Brazil), 19 September, p.D7. Interview with the artist. Portuguese.

Beckett, Andy. 'Is there life after the dead cow?', *The Independent on Sunday*, 27 October, p.18-19, 21-22. Interviews with Turner Prize nominees.

Boogerd van den, Dominic. 'Schijngestalten: De synthetische schilderijen van Gary Hume', *Jong Holland*, no.1, pp.9-14. Dutch.

Buck, Louisa. 'Works in progress', *GQ Magazine*, issue 90, December, pp.86-90. Portraits of five British artists.

Caderno, Dois. 'Gary Hume', *Correio Brazilense* (Brazil), 16 October, p.1. Review of São Paulo Bienal. Portuguese.

Chant, Katharine. 'Gary Hume', *Exeter Express & Echo*, 17 January, p.19. Review of exhibition at Spacex Gallery, Exeter, 1996.

Floravante, Celso. 'Grã-Bretanha traz Gary Hume de Sao Paulo', *Folha de São Paulo*, 10 August, p.4.

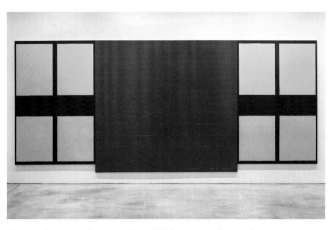

Present from an Octogenarian, 1991, gloss paint on four MDF
panels, 208.3 × 498 cm

Stop, 1991, gloss paint on three formica panels, 218.4 × 536 cm
and *Present from an Octogenarian*, 1991, gloss paint on four MDF
panels, 208.3 × 498 cm. Installation view, *Gary Hume: Recent
Paintings*, Daniel Weinberg Gallery, Santa Monica, 1992

Review of São Paulo Bienal. Portuguese.
Fortes, Márcia. 'XXIII Bienal Internacional de São
Paulo', *frieze*, issue 32, January/February, 1997,
p.76.
Garnett, Robert. 'Beyond the hype', *Art Monthly*,
no.195, April, pp.43-4.
Gonçalves Filho, Antonio. 'Gary Hume', *O Estado
de São Paulo*, 3 October. Review of the São Paulo
Bienal. Portuguese.
Graham-Dixon, Andrew. 'Spreading the Word',
The Independent, 12 November, pp.4-5. Review of
the *Turner Prize 1996*.
Herbert, Martin and Mark Sanders. 'Next stop
Barbados', *Dazed & Confused Magazine*, issue 26,
pp.54-57. Interview with the artist.
MacMillan, Ian. 'Bold with beauty', *Modern
Painters*, vol.9, no.4, Winter 1996, pp.36-39.
MacRitchie, Lynn. 'Their Brilliant Careers', *Art In
America*, vol.84, no.4, April, pp.80-84, 132.
Review of *Brilliant!: New Art from London* at the
Walker Arts Center, Minneapolis, 1995.
Parkett, no.48, pp.12-39. Texts by Lionel Bovier,
Douglas Fogle & Gregor Muir. Special feature on
Gary Hume.

1997   Adams, Brooks. 'Gary Hume', *Elle Decor* (US
edition), October/November, pp.72-78.
Collings, Matthew. 'The New Establishment',
Independent on Sunday, 31 August, pp.9-14.
Coomer, Martin. 'The Jerwood Painting Prize',
Time Out, no.1416, 8-5 October, p.51. Review of
Jerwood Painting Prize, 1997.

Cork, Richard. 'Teasing and Pleasing in full colour',
The Times, 21 January 1997, p.35a. Review of
exhibition at The Saatchi Gallery, London, 1997.
Garratt, Sheryl. 'Gary Hume', *The Face*, vol.3,
no.1, February, pp.76-80.
Gayford, Martin. 'Painted into a corner', *The Daily
Telegraph*, 1 October, p.16. Review of *Jerwood
Painting Prize*, 1997.
Glueck, Grace. 'Gary Hume', *The New York Times*,
Friday, 16 May. Review of exhibition at Matthew
Marks Gallery, New York, 1997.
Ingleby, Richard. 'Fiona Rae, Gary Hume', *The
Independent*, 24 January, Arts p.23. Review of
exhibition at The Saatchi Gallery, London, 1997.
'It's a Sensation but is it Art?', *Time Out*, no.1412,
10-17 September. 34 page supplement on
Sensation and young British artists. Texts by
Martin Herbert, Sarah Kent, Ian MacMillan &
Elaine Paterson.
Kent, Sarah. 'Access Denied', *Time Out*, no.1377,
8-15 January, p.48. Review of exhibition at The
Saatchi Gallery, London, 1997.
Lambirth, Andrew. 'Time to put a little gloss on
the presentation', *The Independent*, 30 September,
Features section p.19. Article on the *Jerwood
Painting Prize*, 1997.
Morrissey, Simon. 'Fiona Rae, Gary Hume',
Contemporary Visual Arts, no.14, pp.64-65. Review
of exhibition at The Saatchi Gallery, London, 1997.
Reynolds, Nigel. 'From Sensation to £30,000 prize',
The Daily Telegraph, 30 September, p.10. Article

Incubus, 1991, oil and gloss paint on three formica panels, 238.7 × 383.5 cm, and *More Fucking Values*, 1991, oil and gloss paint on formica panel, 221 × 170 cm

Jim, 1991, oil and gloss paint on four formica panels, 238.8 × 528.3 cm and *Little Jim*, 1991, oil and gloss paint on formica panel, 238.7 × 150 cm. Installation view, *Gary Hume: New Paintings*, Matthew Marks Gallery, New York, 1992

on the artist winning the *Jerwood Painting Prize*, 1997.

1998 'Art's New Establishment', The *Independent on Sunday*, 31 August, Review section pp.9-14. Texts by Annabella Auerbach, Matthew Collings, Richard Ingleby & Rosanna de Lisle.

Baker, Lindsay. 'The Beauty Bomber', *The Guardian*, 2 May, pp.40-43.

Buck, Louisa. 'London Calling: Gary Hume at Sadler's Wells', *The Art Newspaper*, vol.10, no.85, October, p.53. Article on commission for Sadler's Wells Theatre, London, 1998.

Collings, Matthew. 'Sensation', *Artforum*, vol.36, no.5, January, pp.94-95. Review of *Sensation*, Royal Academy of Arts, London, 1997.

Falconer, Morgan. 'Beneath the surface of a shy superstar of painting', *Highbury & Islington Express*, 30 October, Arts & Leisure section, p.27. Article on commission for Sadlers Wells Theatre, 1998.

Fulcher, Dawn. 'The Enchanted Garden', *Contemporary Visual Arts*, issue 19, p.90. Review of *The Enchanted Garden*, Salisbury, 1998.

Higgie, Jennifer. 'Gary Hume', *Bijutsu Techo* (Tokyo), November, pp.10-15. Interview with the artist. Japanese.

Ingleby, Richard. 'Art', *The Independent*, 15 September. Review of installation outside the Hayward Gallery, London, 1998.

Lee, Sook-Kyung. 'A look at Life and Art: British Contemporary Art Exhibition at the National Museum of Contemporary Art', *Woolgan Misool* (Korea), August, pp.54-57. Text in Korean.

Millard, Rosie. 'Summer Pudding', *Art Review*, July/August, pp.48-49. Review of London summer exhibitions.

Mi-Lui, Kim. 'New Era in British Contemporary Art on show in Seoul', *The Korean Times*, 4 September, p.2. Korean text.

Pollack, Barbara. 'Green Cards: yBa's in the US', *Art Monthly*, no.214, March, pp.44-45.

Redhead, David. 'When Gary met Georgie', *Elle Decoration* (UK edition), November, pp.94-101. Feature on the artist.

Relyea, Lane, 'Virtually Formal', *Artforum*, vol.37, no.1, September, pp.126-133, 173.

Sladen, Mark. 'The South Bank Show: Young British Artists', *tate: The Art Magazine*, issue 15, Summer, p.78. Review of television programme *The South Bank Show*, 1998.

Ville de, Nicholas. 'Ways of Seeing and the Pleasures of the Visual', *Contemporary Visual Arts*, issue 18, pp.56-62.

1999 Higgins, Rita. 'Mixing it in the art world', *The Sunday Times*, 7 March, magazine section, p.17.

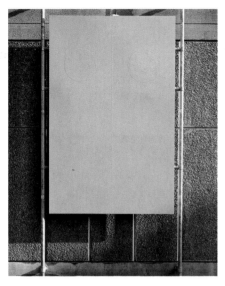

Outside Door Painting, 1998, gloss paint on aluminium panel, 305 × 200 cm

Outside Door Paintings, 1998, gloss paint on aluminium panels, each 305 × 200 cm. Installation view, *Turnaround: Inside Out at the Hayward*, Hayward Gallery, London, 1998

FURTHER REFERENCES

Artists. Tate Gallery Publishing, London, 1999. Text by Mel Gooding. Photographs by Gautier Deblonde.

Buck, Louisa. *Moving Targets: A user's guide to British Art now*, Tate Gallery Publishing, London, 1997

Button, Virginia. *The Turner Prize*, Tate Gallery Publications, London, 1997.

Collings, Matthew. *Blimey! From Bohemia to Britpop: The London Artworld from Francis Bacon to Damien Hirst*, 21, Cambridge, 1997.

Collings, Matthew. *This is Modern Art*, Weidenfeld & Nicholson, London, 1999.

Cork, Richard, Sarah Kent and Dick Price. *Young British Art: The Saatchi Decade*, Booth-Clibborn Editions, London, 1999.

Gillick, Liam and Andrew Renton (eds.). *Technique Anglaise: Current Trends in British Art*, Thames and Hudson Ltd., London, 1991.

Kent, Sarah. *Shark Infested Waters: The Saatchi Collection of British Art in the 90s*, Zwemmer, London, 1994.

Loock, Ulrich. *Jahresbericht des Veriens Kunsthalle Bern*, Kunsthalle Berne, 1995. German.

Shand Kydd, Johnnie. *Spit Fire. Photographs from the Art World London 1996/97*, Thames & Hudson, London in association with Violette Editions, USA, 1997.

Young British Art: The Saatchi Decade, Booth-Clibborn Editions, London, 1999.

VIDEOGRAPHY

The Hanging Picnic, an Illuminations production for LWT, 1995

The Turner Prize, an Illuminations production for Channel 4, 1996

This is Modern Art, an Oxford Television Company production for Channel 4, 1999

Death of a Curator, an Illuminations production for BBC 2, 1999

COLLECTIONS

Arts Council Collection, Hayward Gallery, London
Astrup Fearnley Museet for Moderne Kunst, Oslo
Bonnefantenmuseum, Maastricht
The British Council
DESTE Foundation for Contemporary Art, Athens
NatWest Group Art Collection, London
Saatchi Gallery, London
San Francisco Museum of Modern Art, San Francisco
Tate Gallery, London
Kunstmuseum Wolfsburg, Wolfsburg
Yale Center for British Art, New Haven

Gary Hume is represented by Jay Jopling (London) and by Matthew Marks Gallery, New York

CATALOGUE LIST

WATER PAINTING, 1999
gloss paint on aluminium panel
305 × 241.3 cm
Courtesy Jay Jopling, London

WATER PAINTING, 1999
gloss paint on aluminium panel
305 × 241.3 cm
Courtesy Jay Jopling, London

WATER PAINTING, 1999
gloss paint on aluminium panel
305 × 241.3 cm
Courtesy Matthew Marks
Gallery, New York

WATER PAINTING, 1999
gloss paint on aluminium panel
305 × 241.3 cm
Courtesy Jay Jopling, London

RED ANGELS, 1998
gloss paint on aluminium panel
200 × 162.7 cm
Private collection, courtesy
Jay Jopling, London

YELLOW ANGELS, 1999
gloss paint on aluminium panel
305 × 241.3 cm
Courtesy Matthew Marks
Gallery, New York

FALLING, 1995
gloss paint on aluminium panel
200.2 × 124.8 cm
Private collection, London

CAVE PAULINE, 1998
gloss paint on aluminium panel
208.2 × 116.8 cm
Private collection, London

PAULINE, 1996
gloss paint on aluminium panel
208.2 × 116.8 cm
Eric and Louise Franck, London

BIRDSONG, 1998
gloss paint on aluminium panel
208.3 × 116.2 cm
Private collection, Mike Meiré,
Cologne

KATE, 1996
gloss paint and paper on
aluminium panel
208.2 × 116.7 cm
Private collection, London

WIDOW, 1997
gloss, oil and charcoal on
aluminium panel
221 × 170 cm
Private collection, courtesy
Matthew Marks Gallery,
New York

CERITH, 1997
gloss paint on aluminium panel
198 × 150 cm
Collection of Joe and Marie
Donnelly, courtesy Matthew
Marks Gallery, New York

FOUR FEET IN THE GARDEN,
1995
gloss paint on aluminium panel
221 × 170 cm
Arts Council Collection,
Hayward Gallery, London

FRANCIS, 1997
gloss paint on aluminium panel
163 × 163 cm
Private collection, courtesy
Matthew Marks Gallery,
New York

BLACKBIRD, 1998
gloss paint on aluminium panel
234 × 164 cm
Private collection, London

FUNNY GIRL, 1995
gloss paint on aluminium panel
198 × 150 cm
Private collection, London

GARDEN PAINTING NO.1, 1996
gloss paint on aluminium panel
221 × 170 cm
Kunstmuseum Wolfsburg

SCARED, 1999
gloss paint on aluminium panel
200 × 162.5 cm
Courtesy Matthew Marks
Gallery, New York

YELLOW HAIR, 1995
gloss paint on wood panel
199.5 × 122.5 cm
Private collection, London

NEST I, 1998
gloss paint on aluminium panel
201 × 162.5 cm
Kunstmuseum Wolfsburg

NEST II, 1998
gloss paint on aluminium panel
200 × 162.5 cm
Mr and Mrs Sidney Kahn

SNOWMAN, 1996
gloss paint on aluminium panel
201 × 160.5 cm
Courtesy the artist

NEST III, 1998
gloss paint on aluminium panel
200.2 × 162.5 cm
Courtesy Matthew Marks
Gallery, New York

GARDEN PAINTING NO.3, 1996
gloss paint on aluminium panel
198 × 150 cm
Kunstmuseum Wolfsburg

BIRD ON A BRANCH, 1998
gloss paint on aluminium panel
200.8 × 160.2 cm
Joel and Sherry Mallin,
New York

POOR THING, 1994
gloss paint on aluminium panel
198 × 150 cm
Collection of George P. Mills,
New York

MESSIAH, 1998
gloss paint on aluminium panel
208.5 × 116.8 cm
Private collection, courtesy
Jay Jopling, London

LADY PARKER
(AFTER HOLBEIN), 1998
gloss paint on aluminium panel
233.7 × 163.8 cm
Guy & Annushka Shani, London

POLAR BEAR, 1994
gloss paint on aluminium panel
198 × 150 cm
Private collection, Berne

PHOTO CREDITS:

David Batchelor
Don Brown
Bob Goadawaagaan
Tom Haartsen
Gary Hume
Bill Jacobson
Anthony Oliver
Orcutt & Van der Putten
Susan Ormerod
Douglas M Parker Studio
John Riddy
Caroline Rose
Simon Vogel
Stephen White

SPECIAL THANKS TO:

Judy Adam
Andrea Addison
Dick Alford
Martine d'Anglejan-Chatillon
Tim Baker
Nick Banks
Brad Barnes
Jackee Bennett
Natalie Bethell
Simon Bill
Irene Bradbury
Don Brown
Krzysztof Cieszkowski
Jarvis Cocker
Mario & Mirta Codognato
Sadie Coles
Mark Cooper
Linda Copperwheat
Sarah Crompton
Liz Crookall
Sarah den Dikken
Frédérique Dolivet
Francesco Donadio
Richard Dorment
Caroline Douglas
Candida Doyle
Meg Duff
Ann Gallagher
Paul Gent
Sophie Grieg
Zoë Griffiths
Andrew Gwilliams
Ella O'Halloran
Sue Hamston
Pru Harris
Keith Hartley
Richard Hawley
Georgie Hopton
Tim Hunt
Jay Jopling
John Kieffer
Catherine Lampert

Michel Letendrie
Honey Luard
Steve Mackey
Dave Magliano
Matthew Marks
Suvi McCreadie
Andrew Missingham
Gregor Muir
Judith Nesbitt
Mary Openshaw
Jeffrey Peabody
Clive Phillpot
Linda Porter
Sophie Price
Jacqueline Rapmund
Richard Riley
Brett Rogers
Julia Royse
Karsten Schubert
Nigel Semmens
Annushka Shani
Jo Soughan
Catherine Starling
Clare Storey
Antonio Tomassini
Gijs van Tuyl
William Wallis
Ben Weaver
Mark Webber